D1537150

UNOFFICIAL
ANCESTRY.COM
WORKBOOK

UNOFFICIAL
ANCESTRY.COM
WORKBOOK

A How-To Manual
for Tracing Your
Family Tree on the
#1 Genealogy Website

NANCY HENDRICKSON

FAMILY
TREE
BOOKS

CINCINNATI, OHIO
shopfamilytree.com

CONTENTS

INTRODUCTION

Like many genealogy buffs, I found my way to family research via my grandmothers. Both spun tales that would have captivated any kid, and those stories stayed with me for decades.

One of my first genealogy memories is of ordering records from the National Archives when I was in my early teens. I was thrilled to discover that Grandma's story about her Civil War ancestor was accurate; from then on, I was hooked.

In 1986, I logged onto CompuServe, a computer network where I found my first online genealogy community. The idea of being able to instantly communicate with someone across the globe—and to find even a handful of genealogy records—was mind-boggling. Since then, I've seen Internet genealogy grow from a tiny seed to a full-blown forest. And leading the way into that forest was first RootsWeb—and then Ancestry.com.

Through my work with *Family Tree Magazine* **<www.familytreemagazine.com>**, I wrote extensively about Internet genealogy, including many of the properties that eventually came under the Ancestry.com umbrella, such as Fold3 **<www.fold3.com>** and Find a Grave **<www.findagrave.com>**.

Then I wrote the *Unofficial Guide to Ancestry.com* **<www.shopfamilytree.com/unofficial-guide-to-ancestry>**, with the first edition released in 2014 and updated over the next couple of years. This workbook is meant to be used either as a stand-alone guide to Ancestry.com or as a companion to the original book.

While writing my two Ancestry.com books, I discovered much about the site's thousands of collections and how best to attack specific research problems. And by using this workbook, you can look over my shoulder as I attempt to solve real-life genealogy puzzles using Ancestry.com and its resources, then you can use the same techniques to work on your own family's history.

HOW TO USE THIS BOOK

Each chapter focuses on a specific record type or Ancestry.com resource: censuses, vital records, military records, immigration, maps, images, newspapers, publications, social history, and DNA. In each chapter, you'll find:

- an **overview** of the collections for the record type
- **exercises** that illustrate common research goals and take you step-by-step through how to use Ancestry.com to complete them
- a list of **search strategies** to use in queries
- **forms and worksheets** to help you plan, develop, record, and analyze your research and data

The appendices in the back of this workbook include more tools and worksheets for you to use in your research, such as general genealogy forms and census abstract templates. For example, you can create your own step-by-step search (like the ones at the end of each chapter) using the Your Ancestry.com Search Worksheets in appendix B searches. You can download these—and all the other worksheets in

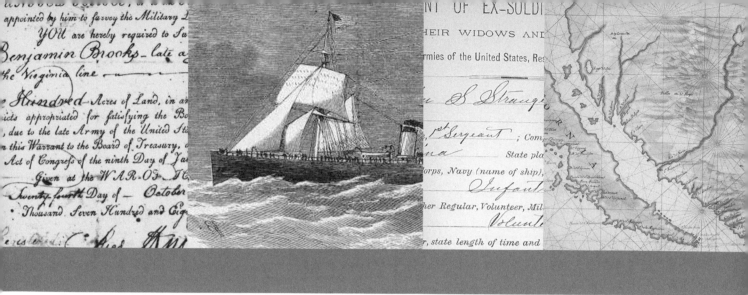

this workbook—from <ftu.familytreemagazine.com/unofficial-ancestry-workbook>.

Read chapter 1 before you begin any of the other sections. This chapter describes how to conduct research using Ancestry.com's general search form and the Card Catalog, plus how to identify when to use each research tool. Once you understand how both approaches work, you're good to go. It's not imperative that you read the rest of the book in any particular order; just jump to the chapter that addresses the type of record you want to search.

GETTING GREAT RESULTS

It's my hope that you search along with me through the exercises. This way, you'll see why I made certain search decisions, and why you might make different ones. Successful research, after all, is really about the thought process that goes into tackling a problem.

But If I could sit next to you during an Ancestry.com search, the one piece of advice I'd offer is to be a flexible thinker. Genealogy information has a habit of finding its way into strange and wondrous places. What you think you'll find in one record magically pops up somewhere else.

Be open to possibilities and think laterally. For me, that means isolating one individual and conjuring up every possible record or document where he might appear: school yearbooks, newspapers, estate sales, state censuses, employee records, property taxes, county histories, and so forth.

In addition, I'd encourage you to realize how much information can be hiding in plain sight on a document or how much a record type might have changed over time. For example: If you can't find a marriage record, did you check the census? Some census records show whether the person was married within the year; others actually indicate the number of years a couple has been married. Or if you've ever wondered why a young family member wasn't living with his parents, check the probate files. It's possible he was an orphan and now living under the care of an uncle or another family member.

One way to think about your search strategy is this: If someone two hundred years in the future were trying to track you down, where would they look? What records have you left behind that a researcher could seek out? The more a researcher understands about an ancestor's life, the better equipped he or she is to coax that relative out of hiding.

As you research your own family, it's my hope that the exercises and search strategies you'll find here will help you break down long-time brick walls or newly found challenges.

As Ancestry.com continues to acquire more genealogy services and digitize millions more records, it cements its continued role as must-use resource for researchers. And whether you use it for a month or for years, I wish you happy searching!

SEARCH AND THE CARD CATALOG

Ancestry.com has made searching for ancestors super simple. With fill-in-the-blank forms for major categories of records like immigration, military, and birth, you can easily go directly to the category of records you need and begin your search. But there's also a second way of finding your ancestors: the Card Catalog. It's less used than the standard search function, but it can be far more effective in many instances.

In this chapter, I'll show you how to get the most out of both approaches.

SEARCH

Ancestry.com's primary (and most famous) research tool is its Search form. Ancestry.com Search is your gateway to the website's more than 17 billion records, but you may feel lost in the face of all those records. This section will help you feel confident using the Search form to drill down into Ancestry.com's massive stockpile of records and discover research gems.

When you click Search, located at the top of all Ancestry.com pages (image **A**), you can select which category of records collections you'd like to investi-gate. For now, click All Collections; we'll discuss the other categories in detail in later chapters. On the All Collections page <search.ancestry.com>, a search form pops up (image **B**), inviting you to enter the name of the person you're seeking along with any relevant information such as date of birth or place lived.

Using this general, All Collections search box tells the system to search everything on the site: all records collections, user-submitted family trees and ancestor profiles, and collections of historical maps and photos. By searching so many resources at once, you're casting a wide net and will probably find relevant family records. However, you may also get thousands upon thousands of search results and bury the information you need beneath tons of irrel-evant records.

If you choose to use this form, you have a few ways of narrowing search parameters. At the bottom of the form, you'll see a pull-down arrow under Collection Focus. Use this to select the country of research inter-est; for example, selecting Scotland from the pull-down forces Ancestry.com to return only results that come from Scotland.

A

Ancestry.com's main toolbar (accessible at the top of most pages) allows users to navigate the site's major features.

Search

First & Middle Name(s)

Last Name

Place your ancestor might have lived

City, County, State, Country

Birth Year

SEARCH Show fewer options ^ ▢ Match all terms exactly

Add event: Birth Marriage Death Lived In Any Event More ⌄

Add family member: Father Mother Sibling Spouse Child

Keyword

Occupation, street address, etc.

Gender
-- Select --

Race/Nationality

Collection Focus
United States

☑ Historical Records   ☑ Family Trees
☑ Stories & Publications   ☑ Photos & Maps

SEARCH Clear search

Recent Searches   **+ SEE MORE**

Smith | Winters | hendrickson | winter

Explore by Location

| USA | UK & IRELAND | EUROPE | CANADA | AUSTRALIA & NZ |

United States

Recent additions include:

- 1940 United States Federal Census - **New**
- 1930 United States Federal Census - **Updated**
- U.S. City Directories (Beta)

Alabama	Florida	Louisiana	Nebraska	Oklahoma	Vermont
Alaska	Georgia	Maine	Nevada	Oregon	Virginia
Arizona	Hawaii	Maryland	New Hampshire	Pennsylvania	Washington
Arkansas	Idaho	Massachusetts	New Jersey	Rhode Island	West Virginia
California	Illinois	Michigan	New Mexico	South Carolina	Wisconsin
Colorado	Indiana	Minnesota	New York	South Dakota	Wyoming
Connecticut	Iowa	Mississippi	North Carolina	Tennessee	USA
Delaware	Kansas	Missouri	North Dakota	Texas	
District of Columbia	Kentucky	Montana	Ohio	Utah	

Recently Viewed Collections   **+ SEE MORE**

1920 United States Federal Census
Public Member Trees
Public Member Photos & Scanned Documents

Special Collections   **+ CARD CATALOG**

Historical Records

Birth, Marriage & Death
Birth, Baptism & Christening
Marriage & Divorce
Death, Burial, Cemetery & Obituaries

Census & Voter Lists
U.S. Federal Census Collection
UK Census Collection
Canadian Census Collection
More...

Immigration & Travel
Passenger Lists
Citizenship & Naturalization Records
Border Crossings & Passports
More...

Military
Draft, Enlistment and Service
Casualties
Soldier, Veteran & Prisoner Rolls & Lists
More...

Schools, Directories & Church Histories
City & Area Directories
Professional & Organizational Directories
Church Histories & Records
More...

Tax, Criminal, Land & Wills
U.S. Wills and Probates
Land Records
Court, Governmental & Criminal Records
More...

Reference, Dictionaries & Almanacs
General Reference Materials
Research Guides & Finding Aids
Dictionaries & Encyclopedias
More...

Family Trees

Public Member Trees
More...

Stories & Publications

Stories, Memories & Histories
Newspapers
Periodicals & Magazines

Photos & Maps

Pictures
Maps, Atlases & Gazetteers

Special Collections

African American Collections
American Indian Records
Jewish Family History
New York 400th Anniversary
Quaker Collections

VIEW ALL IN CARD CATALOG

You can search Ancestry.com's entire trove of records using the All Collections form—though the sheer number of results can sometimes be overwhelming and hide the most relevant record matches.

In addition, checkboxes for four types of collections will appear:

1. Historical Records
2. Family Trees
3. Stories & Publications
4. Photos & Maps

By default, all four are checked. However, you can narrow by collection, drastically reducing the number of results. If you only want to search through Photos & Maps, for example, deselect the other three categories.

When to Use the General Search Form

There are only a few instances in which I suggest using the general search form.

The first is when you're just getting started in family tree research. If you only know a little about your family or have limited knowledge about genealogy in general, start with this form. Your search will likely result in thousands or even tens of thousands of results. While this sounds like a godsend for your research, some of your results will only appear because

C

First & Middle Name(s): galen

Last Name: cave

☐ Exact...   ☐ Exact...

Place your ancestor might have lived:

Birth Year: 1800

☐ Exact +/-...

SEARCH   Show fewer options ^   ☐ Match all terms exactly

Add event: Birth   Marriage   Death   Lived In   Any Event   More ∨

Birth   Year: 1800   Location: Virginia, USA   ✕

☐ Exact +/-...   ☐ Exact to...

Add family member: Father   Mother   Sibling   Spouse   Child

Keyword: Occupation, street address, etc.

Gender: -- Select --

Race/Nationality:

Collection Focus: United States

☑ Historical Records   ☑ Family Trees
☑ Stories & Publications   ☑ Photos & Maps

SEARCH   Clear search

On the All Collections search form, you can select which types of results you'd like to see. Leaving all four (Historical Records, Family Trees, Stories & Publications, and Photos & Maps) casts the widest net.

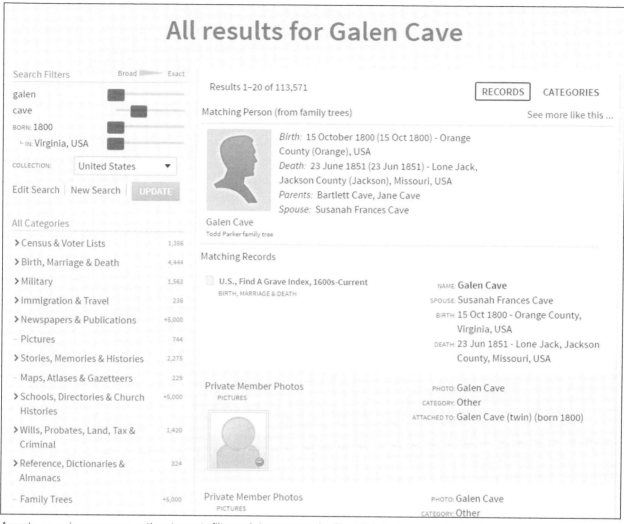

All results for Galen Cave

Search Filters   Broad ▬ Exact

galen

cave

BORN: 1800

└ IN: Virginia, USA

COLLECTION: United States ▾

Edit Search | New Search | **UPDATE**

All Categories

❯ Census & Voter Lists	1,356
❯ Birth, Marriage & Death	4,444
❯ Military	1,563
❯ Immigration & Travel	236
❯ Newspapers & Publications	+5,000
– Pictures	744
❯ Stories, Memories & Histories	2,275
– Maps, Atlases & Gazetteers	229
❯ Schools, Directories & Church Histories	+5,000
❯ Wills, Probates, Land, Tax & Criminal	1,420
❯ Reference, Dictionaries & Almanacs	324
– Family Trees	+5,000

Results 1–20 of 113,571   **RECORDS**   CATEGORIES

Matching Person (from family trees)   See more like this ...

Birth: 15 October 1800 (15 Oct 1800) - Orange County (Orange), USA
Death: 23 June 1851 (23 Jun 1851) - Lone Jack, Jackson County (Jackson), Missouri, USA
Parents: Bartlett Cave, Jane Cave
Spouse: Susanah Frances Cave

Galen Cave
Todd Parker family tree

Matching Records

📄 U.S., Find A Grave Index, 1600s-Current
BIRTH, MARRIAGE & DEATH

NAME: **Galen Cave**
SPOUSE: Susanah Frances Cave
BIRTH: 15 Oct 1800 - Orange County, Virginia, USA
DEATH: 23 Jun 1851 - Lone Jack, Jackson County, Missouri, USA

Private Member Photos
PICTURES

PHOTO: Galen Cave
CATEGORY: Other
ATTACHED TO: Galen Cave (twin) (born 1800)

Private Member Photos
PICTURES

PHOTO: Galen Cave
CATEGORY: Other

Ancestry.com gives you many options to use to filter and view your results. The All Collections search will return many results, often in the hundreds of thousands.

---

the search engine is casting the widest possible net over all of its billions of records. To put it another way: The search engine will present people not even remotely related to you. A search like this will take some patience on your part because of the number of irrelevant results, but it's a good starting place.

The second instance in which the general search function excels is if you've been searching, without success, for an ancestor who stubbornly remains hidden. Even with my extensive background in genealogy research, I'll often strike out and still not find what I'm looking for after trying every possible combination of advanced search techniques. When I hit this kind of brick wall, I'll turn to the general search form. Hopefully, some other researcher will have posted a tiny kernel of information that will open up another search

path, and the general search's wide net might be the perfect tool to pull that tiny kernel into the light.

The third time this form is useful is when you're just getting started on a previously unresearched family line. You may know the names and approximate dates for a few generations back, but your general knowledge of the particular family might be slim. Using the general form allows you to get a sense of what research has already been done and what you might expect to find.

Let me show you what I mean. I know that I have a peripheral ancestor (a many-times-removed cousin) named Galen Cave, who was born in Virginia in 1800 and died in Lone Jack, Missouri. I have a few fragments of information about him, but not enough to feel confident going back much further in his family tree. Using the general search form, I entered only his name and date and place of birth. I also chose to leave all of the categories at the bottom of the form selected (image **C**). When I clicked the Search button, I ended up with 113,571 results. Obviously, there's insufficient room in an image to show you all of the results, but image **D** will suffice.

Try this search along with me, because I think it will give you the opportunity to see if your next steps match my own search decisions. Your results may be much better than mine! Go ahead and do that initial search, then return once you've finished.

Among my first results, four things stood out:

1. The first match came from a public family tree, which tells me this user is also researching the Cave family. Contacting that user could be one of my first steps.

2. The reference to the online, crowd-sourced Find A Grave <www.findagrave.com> indicates that someone has located Cave's burial site, meaning that someone has also been researching Cave's death.

3. In addition to telling me that yet another person is working on this family line, the Find A Grave result also indicates Cave died in Lone Jack, Missouri. Given that (and the fact that my own research places this part of the family in Lone Jack), I can assume this is a match.

4. This relative has many matches in many record categories, opening up additional areas of research. On the left side of the search results page, you'll find a list of all the categories that include Cave results. This is the area to scrutinize depending on what you're trying to find. In my case, I just wanted a starting point for Cave research, so I concentrated on the person who uploaded the public tree. (Indeed: By reviewing the Public Family Tree, I learned Galen Cave's county of birth, the names of his parents, and information about the birth of his child.) But I will also keep a record of the search results, as they'll help whenever I delve into specific records categories such as census registers or military records.

Record Categories

Ancestry.com has divided its records collections into large "buckets" that we'll be calling categories. For instance, some collections (such as passenger lists and naturalization papers) go in the Immigration category while others (such as wills) go in the Probate category. Let's review what large categories you're able to search in addition to the site's general Search form. If you click Search on the main menu at the top of page, you'll get a drop-down box of the many ways you can search (image **E**):

- All Collections: This is the general search form (discussed earlier in this chapter) that will search all collections and records.

- Census & Voter Lists: This will limit your searches to all of the collections in the Card Catalog that relate to these two topics. (See chapter 2.)

E

TREES   SEARCH   DNA

All Collections

Census & Voter Lists

Birth, Marriage & Death

Immigration & Travel

Public Member Trees

Military

Card Catalog

Member Directory

Ancestry.com has search forms for each of its major records categories.

Suggested Records

The programming behind Ancestry.com is pretty smart. It takes the information you say you're looking for and intuitively suggests specific places for you to search. Here's how that works:

After clicking on Search, choose the category Census & Voter Lists. That will bring up the Census & Voter Lists form. It will also display a new list, along the right side of the page, of other possible places for you to search for census and voter list information.

Keep in mind that these links are served up as suggestions before you even begin your search. Each of these links will drive you deeper into the site and into even more choices. If you click on the "U.S. Federal Census Collection" link, for example, you'll next be given the choice to search all of the census collections, or individually by census date.

But what happens once you type in a name and begin your search? Let's see. Using the Census & Voter Lists form, I entered the information I had on Galen Cave. The search results served up more than one thousand hits.

Once I click on a result, like the first one from the 1840 US census, Ancestry.com serves up yet another list of suggestions ("Suggested Records") located on the right side of the page) that it thinks are pertinent to my search.

Ancestry.com's system is built to help you find records, even in places you may not think to look. A great example is the North Carolina Marriage Index suggestion for Galen Cave. It wasn't on my radar as a search target, but Ancestry.com's intuitive programming pulled it as relevant to my search.

Narrow by Category

U.S. Federal Census Collection

U.K. Census Collection

Canadian Census Collection, 1851-1916

1700s Censuses

1800s Censuses

1900s Censuses

Featured data collections

1940 United States Federal Census `FREE`

Australia, Electoral Rolls, 1903-1980 `UPDATED`

U.S., Indian Census Rolls, 1885-1940

`VIEW ALL IN CARD CATALOG`

Before you begin your search, Ancestry.com will recommend collections based on what record type you're researching.

Suggested Records

North Carolina, Marriage Index, 1741-2004
Galin Cave

1850 United States Federal Census
Garlon Cave

North Carolina, Index to Marriage Bonds, 1741-1868
Galin Cave

Web: Missouri, Find A Grave Index, 1812-2012
Galen Cave

Once you click on a search result, Ancestry.com provides a list of suggested records that can open new paths of research.

- Birth, Marriage & Death: Use this form if you want to limit searches to records related to these vital records. (See chapter 3.)

- Immigration & Travel: Select this group for any searches relevant to finding an immigrant ancestor or resources such as passports. (See chapter 5.)

- Public Member Trees: This search will take you specifically to the family trees that have been uploaded by Ancestry.com members. (See chapter 7.)

- Military: This searches all of the military collections, including draft registrations, muster rolls, and pension applications. (See chapter 4.)

We'll discuss each major category of records and how to use them in later chapters, but for now just know that these categories allow you to search large amounts of similarly focused records at once.

THE CARD CATALOG

With the few exceptions mentioned earlier, most of my Ancestry.com searches begin at the Card Catalog <search.ancestry.com/search/cardcatalog>. I think the Card Catalog is Ancestry.com's most powerful search tool, yet it may not be something you've ever used. To access it, click the Search tab from the top menu bar, then find Card Catalog as one of the last options.

First, you need to know that the Card Catalog isn't for locating your ancestors. It's for locating *collections* that might contain your ancestors—and not just any old collections, but those that are most relevant to your search and have the highest odds for a successful search.

Why am I such a proponent of using the Card Catalog? Because it narrows your search down to the most relevant collections for a specific search. When you use the general search form (or even one of the more specific record forms), Ancestry.com sends its robot search team out through its tens of thousands of collections and billions of records. It then returns anything it thinks has even a slight possibility of matching your search request. Most of the time, you'll benefit from a more targeted search, and that begins with the Card Catalog.

Card Catalog Filters

When you use the Card Catalog, you can set up search parameters that force the Ancestry.com system to pull only the collections that are relevant to your search. This is done by setting up filters. When you first click over to the Card Catalog, you can search through every single record and collection you want sorted by popularity (image **F**), collection title, record count, date updated, or date added.

In addition, running along the left side of the page are filters for:
- title
- keyword(s)
- collection (a.k.a. category; see image **G**)
- location
- dates
- languages

This may not seem like a lot of filters at first. However, upon clicking on a filter, you'll receive even more options. For example, if you choose USA as a location filter, you'll next have the option of choosing an individual state.

Similarly, if you choose a category such as Stories, Memories & Histories (which will be discussed in more depth in chapter 7), you can filter even further by the subcategories that will appear:
- Family Histories, Journals & Biographies
- Oral Histories & Interviews
- Social & Place Histories
- Society & Organization Histories
- Military Histories
- Royalty, Nobility & Heraldry

See the Quick Guide: Ancestry.com Categories and Subcategories worksheet at the end of this chapter for more on the Card Catalog's categorization system.

Note: The number next to each category and subcategory doesn't represent the number of records in the category. Rather, it represents the number of *collections* in the category. That means if you're interested in oral histories and interviews, you'll find roughly sixteen collections relevant to that category.

If your filtered search returns too many collections to reasonably review, try using the additional filters Title and Keywords.

Card Catalog
Searchable listing of all record collections

Title

Keyword(s)

[SEARCH]   or   Clear All

Filter By Collection

Census & Voter Lists	606
Birth, Marriage & Death	+1000
Military	+1000
Immigration & Travel	503
Newspapers & Publications	+1000
Pictures	39
Stories, Memories & Histories	+1000
Maps, Atlases & Gazetteers	188
Schools, Directories & Church Histories	+1000
Wills, Probates, Land, Tax & Criminal	+1000
Reference, Dictionaries & Almanacs	+1000
Family Trees	10

Filter By Location

Australia	214
Canada	+1000
Europe	+1000
Mexico	160
USA	+1000
Africa	37
Asia	72
North America	+1000
Oceania	266
South America	65

Filter by Dates

1600s	1700s	1800s	1900s
1600s	1700s	1800s	1900s
1610s	1710s	1810s	1910s
1620s	1720s	1820s	1920s
1630s	1730s	1830s	1930s
1640s	1740s	1840s	1940s
1650s	1750s	1850s	1950s
1660s	1760s	1860s	1960s
1670s	1770s	1870s	1970s
1680s	1780s	1880s	1980s
1690s	1790s	1890s	1990s

Filter By Languages

German	+1000
English	+1000

Results 1-25 of 32,701   Sort By [Popularity ▼]

Title	Collection	Records	Activity
Public Member Trees	Family Trees	2,147,483,647	
1940 United States Federal Census	Census & Voter Lists	134,484,648	
U.S. City Directories, 1822-1995	Schools, Directories & Church Histories	1,560,284,731	
1930 United States Federal Census	Census & Voter Lists	124,964,074	
1920 United States Federal Census	Census & Voter Lists	107,684,890	
1900 United States Federal Census	Census & Voter Lists	77,277,539	
U.S., Find A Grave Index, 1600s-Current	Birth, Marriage & Death	135,139,799	
1910 United States Federal Census	Census & Voter Lists	93,627,758	
1880 United States Federal Census	Census & Voter Lists	50,480,843	
1911 England Census	Census & Voter Lists	33,847,719	
1870 United States Federal Census	Census & Voter Lists	40,405,477	
U.S., Social Security Death Index, 1935-2014	Birth, Marriage & Death	94,331,864	
Public Member Photos & Scanned Documents	Pictures	192,069,651	
1860 United States Federal Census	Census & Voter Lists	27,493,972	
England, Select Births and Christenings, 1538-1975	Birth, Marriage & Death	192,725,313	
1850 United States Federal Census	Census & Voter Lists	20,053,649	UPDATED
England & Wales, Civil Registration Marriage Index, 1916-2005	Birth, Marriage & Death	61,960,543	
1901 England Census	Census & Voter Lists	30,598,866	UPDATED
England & Wales, Civil Registration Marriage Index, 1837-1915	Birth, Marriage & Death	32,698,349	
U.S., School Yearbooks, 1880-2012	Schools, Directories & Church Histories	372,439,527	
England & Wales, Civil Registration Birth Index, 1916-2005	Birth, Marriage & Death	71,311,492	
England & Wales, Civil Registration Birth Index, 1837-1915	Birth, Marriage & Death	62,793,107	
British Army WWI Service Records, 1914-1920	Military	3,653,052	
New York, Passenger Lists, 1820-1957	Immigration & Travel	82,920,850	
1891 England Census	Census & Voter Lists	27,127,898	

1   2   ...   11   [>]

The Ancestry.com Card Catalog organizes the site's various collections by topic. You can also view collections by popularity, record count, and more.

Filter By Collection	
Census & Voter Lists	588
Birth, Marriage & Death	+1000
Military	+1000
Immigration & Travel	475
Newspapers & Publications	+1000
Pictures	38
Stories, Memories & Histories	+1000
Maps, Atlases & Gazetteers	188
Schools, Directories & Church Histories	+1000
Wills, Probates, Land, Tax & Criminal	+1000
Reference, Dictionaries & Almanacs	+1000
Family Trees	10

You can filter your Card Catalog search results to include only collections that contain particular kinds of records, such as census and voter lists.

For example, filtering for Stories, Memories & Histories, USA produces more than nineteen thousand results. But what if my search goal is information relating only to the state of Kansas? By placing the word *Kansas* in the Title box, Ancestry.com will selectively return collections that have the word *Kansas* in the title of the collection (image **H**). The search results have gone from nineteen thousand to around 150.

But what if I want to expand my search to collections that include the word *Kansas* within the collection data, but are not specifically from Kansas? By putting *Kansas* as a keyword, the search results soar back to more than seven thousand. That's because Ancestry.com's search engine is pulling in all collections that include Kansas information but were not necessarily created in Kansas. This includes collections like the "Hinshaw Index to Quaker Records" and the "Daughters of the American Revolutionary Lineage Books."

Don't forget to check the date filters, as well. As you can see, you can filter by Century or by Decade. This makes your search so much more accurate when you're searching for people with the same name but who lived generations apart, or if you're searching for records specific to an event. For example, the American Civil War took place from 1861 to 1865; select the 1860s as a filter if you're looking for Civil War-era collections.

Say you want to find the most relevant collections for a Civil War ancestor from Ohio. Here's how you might set up filters:

1. Select Military as a category (1,283 collections).
2. Add USA as a filter (1,073 collections).
3. Filter for 1860s (619).
4. Add Ohio from the list of states (147).
5. Add *Civil War* as a keyword (95).
6. Add *Civil War* as a title instead of a keyword (17).

By filtering, you've ended up with seventeen possible collections instead of 1,283. Once you've filtered down to the seventeen collections, click on each one to search it individually.

Titles and Keywords

Ancestry.com's records categories are big buckets—so how can you find relevant collections within the Card Catalog? The first way is using filters to narrow down the collections to a manageable number. The second way is to use the Title and Keyword(s) search boxes either with filters or on their own.

Fair warning: You may miss out on a collection if you use the Title search box and don't experiment with the words you choose to use, as different combinations of filters, titles, and keywords will produce different results. For example, if you're looking for Methodist church records in Ohio, typing *Ohio church* will get you nineteen collections, while *Ohio Methodist* will return only one.

But here's the really interesting part: If you type *church* in the Title box, then use the filters for USA > Ohio (image **I**), you'll get sixty-six collections! And,

Card Catalog

Searchable listing of all record collections

Title

Kansas

Keyword(s)

SEARCH   or   Clear All

Filter By Collection

Census & Voter Lists   14

Birth, Marriage & Death   44

Results 1-25 of 153   Sort By Popularity ▼

Title	Collection	Records	Activity
📄 Kansas State Census Collection, 1855-1925	Census & Voter Lists	8,238,557	
📄 U.S., Index to Alien Case Files at the National Archives at Kansas City, 1944-2003	Immigration & Travel	350,670	
📄 Kansas, Grand Army of the Republic Post Reports, 1880-1940	Military	563,516	
📄 Kansas, Cemetery Records, 1812-1981	Birth, Marriage & Death	33,123	

Using titles and keywords in a Card Catalog collections search can help you narrow your search to a more manageable number of results.

if you do the same search but add *Methodist* as a keyword (image **J**), you'll get four results. The name of the game here is to experiment with different combinations of filters, keywords, and titles.

Are you wondering why the Wiseman family collection showed up in this Methodist church search? It's because Methodist Episcopal Church of New Salem is the subject of the collection. You can always learn more about any collection by placing your mouse over its name; a new box will pop up giving you more information (image **K**).

If you play around with titles, keywords, and filters long enough, you'll find that various combinations of those three can return unexpected (and sometimes wonderful) results. Like a detective pouring over clues, I keep trying new combinations to deduce (or in this case, locate) the best result.

When to Use the Card Catalog

As we did with the Search form, we should also address when to use the Card Catalog instead of other search forms like the Census & Voter Lists or Birth, Marriage & Death categories.

If you know that you're searching for something specific—like your grandparents in the 1940 census— you should probably go directly to the Census & Voter Lists search form, then drill down for the 1940 census using filters.

But, if you heard family stories about Great-grandpa being in the Army, where would you begin your search? Select Military from the Search drop-down menu to access the Military search page. But when you do this, you're searching through all 1,238 collections relating to military records. Wouldn't it be easier to go to the Card Catalog and narrow down to relevant collections?

I

Title

church

Keyword(s)

SEARCH   or   Clear All

Filter Titles

❌ USA

❌ Ohio

You can use titles or keywords in combination with filters to find relevant collections.

I believe that when you have a clearly defined goal with clearly defined collections (like the 1940 federal census or the Social Security Death Index), then go directly to those search forms. In instances in which you have a specific *search* goal (such as "Find a mention of my grandfather in church records" or "Was my ancestor wounded in the Civil War?") without a clearly defined collection, you should use the Card Catalog.

In every chapter in this workbook (with the exception of chapter 8 on AncestryDNA), I'm going to describe the main categories and subcategories of the Card Catalog, then show you how to filter your results to find specific record types or collections to use in your research. Many of the exercises use the Card Catalog, and I invite you to search along with me. (Some exercises will also cover how and when to use the generic search forms).

J

Title

church

Keyword(s)

methodist

[SEARCH] or Clear All

Filter Titles

❌ USA

❌ Ohio

Results 1-4 of 4

Title

📄 History of the Central Ohio Conference of the Methodist Episcopal Church

📄 The Wiseman family and the old church at New Salem : a brief sketch written by the author for his children and for gifts to a f

📄 History of the Methodist Episcopal Church South in Cumberland, Maryland : from 1866 to 1920

📄 The life and times of George Foster Pierce, D.D., LL.D., bishop of the Methodist Episcopal Church, South : with his sketch of

Experimenting with different combinations of titles, keywords, and filters can produce a myriad of results.

K

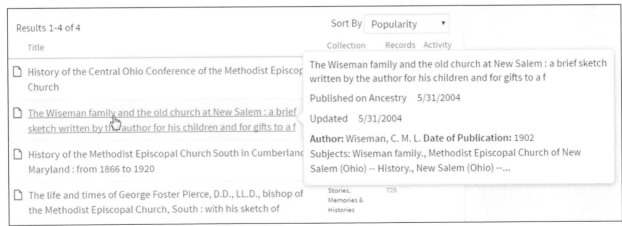

You can learn more about a collection by hovering over its name in your Card Catalog search results.

EXERCISE ① Finding a Photo

RESEARCH GOAL: *Find a photograph of my ancestral town of Milan, Missouri.*

STEP ❶ Find your collection.

If you want to find photos, I suggest you begin your search in three kinds of resources: school yearbooks (more than 370 million records), the Pictures category (thirty-eight collections that include millions of images), and Public Member Trees (more than two billion trees). While other categories of records will have photos, these kinds of records have the most by far. I went to the Card Catalog and filtered for Pictures first, then selected USA > Missouri as additional filters. This returned fifteen results; of those, I felt that "U.S. Historical Postcards" would be a good fit.

STEP ❷ Enter your search terms.

Because I didn't have anything specific in mind, I simply entered the name of the town in the Location search box. This returned more than one hundred thousand results. Why? Because Ancestry.com automatically added Sullivan as the county, so the search was bringing back Milan *and* Sullivan *and* Missouri. I decided to edit the search.

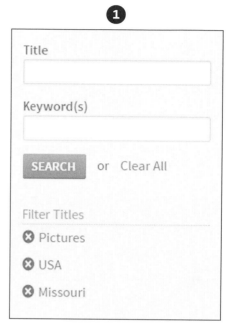

❶

Title

Keyword(s)

SEARCH or Clear All

Filter Titles

❌ Pictures

❌ USA

❌ Missouri

❷

SEARCH ☐ Match all terms exactly

Location

Any Event | Milan, Sullivan, Missouri, USA

☐ Exact to...

Keyword

e.g. pilot or "Flying Tigers" ⌄

Postcard Era

▾

Caption

Location

City | City, County, State, Country

SEARCH Clear search

STEP ❸ Refine your search.

I selected Edit Search on the left (**A**) to return to the search page. This time I made the Location an exact search (**B**). The search now returned three hits, all of which were Milan.

STEP ❹ Search the entire category for more possible results.

Could I have found those images (or other images) with a different search approach? Yes, by searching the entire Pictures category. If you return to the Card Catalog home page and filter for the Pictures category, you'll see a link at the top of the thirty-five-plus collections to search across all of the Pictures category.

What might you find? I could have searched for a specific person, but for now I only wanted to find pictures of Milan. The only thing I entered in the "search entire Pictures Category" form was *Milan Missouri* and I selected the Exact checkbox. This still returned more than fifteen thousand hits. As I skimmed down through them, it was apparent I was finding a lot of images of people on public family trees.

A ❸

B

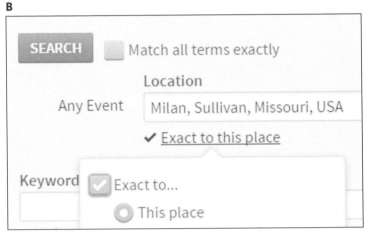

❹

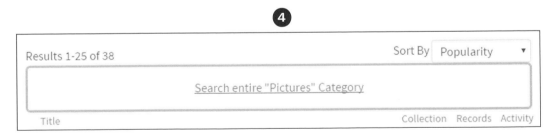

STEP ❺ Filter by collection.

At this point, I went to the left side of the page to see which collections could help me narrow down my results (**A**).

Which collection would you choose? I decided to start with the collection with the smallest (i.e., most manageable) number of records; the numbers you see here are the number of actual records in each collection. Since there were only two in "Member and Institutional Collections," I went there first. Unfortunately, both were articles, so no help there.

How about the "U.S. Family Photo Collection, c. 1850–2000"? As suspected, all five were people pictures, not place pictures. While not helpful to my search, the Sears Catalog (**B**) was interesting because the images were of freight rates between various destinations. (I like filling everyday information into my family tree, so I thought it was cool to discover that in 1924, it cost $1.22 to ship 100 pounds from Chicago to Milan first class.) Besides "U.S., Historical Postcards," the other collections would contain photos of people, so I didn't click there.

What did I learn? First, that I could find the Milan photos in two different ways: by just making what I felt was a logical choice of collections, and also by eliminating other possibilities one by one. Which is best? Both, because while I didn't find any more Milan photos, I did find the little Sears tidbit that will go into my family book.

A

❺

All Categories	
Pictures	
– Public Member Photos & Scanned Documents	10697
– Private Member Photos	3048
– U.S., School Yearbooks, 1880-2012	1366
– Historic Catalogs of Sears, Roebuck and Co., 1896-1993	34
– U.S. Family Photo Collection, c. 1850-2000	5
– U.S., Historical Postcards	3
– Member and Institutional Collections	2
Shortcut Keys ▶	

B

MISSOURI—	
Caruthersville	1.62
Hannibal	.81
Jefferson City	1.08
Kansas City	1.22
Maryville	1.22
Milan	1.22
Nevada	1.40
St. Louis	.79
Salem	1.25
Springfield	1.24
MONTANA—	
Billings	3.75
Glasgow	3.38
Glendive	3.12
Great Falls	3.90
Havre	3.75
Plentywood	3.26

EXERCISE ② Finding an Abstract

RESEARCH GOAL: *Find a record abstract for one of my Snow family members.*

STEP ❶ Identify a record type and find your collection.

Why find an abstract? An abstract contains the pertinent information from a document, such as names, dates, and places. A will abstract, for example, will include the name of the person making the will, the date, the people named in the will, the place, and any other relevant information. An abstract simply *abstracts* material from a document; it does not transcribe it word for word. To start looking for one on Ancestry.com, go to the Card Catalog and type *abstract* in the Title box. You'll see there are less than thirty collections containing abstracts.

STEP ❷ Refine your search.

I typed *abstract* in the Keyword(s) box instead, giving me forty-five results. If I had typed *abstract* in both the Keyword(s) and Title boxes, I would still only get the twenty-eight results from Step 1, because with those terms, I'm telling the system to limit results to the collections containing the word *abstract* in their titles.

❶

Title

abstract

Keyword(s)

SEARCH   or   Clear All

Results 1-25 of 28

Title

☐ Abstract of Graves of Revolutionary Patriots

☐ New Jersey, Abstract of Wills, 1670-1817

❷

Title

Keyword(s)

abstract

SEARCH   or   Clear All

Results 1-25 of 45

Title

☐ Abstract of Graves of Revolutionary Patriots

☐ New Jersey, Abstract of Wills, 1670-1817

STEP ❸ Review your results.

As I was looking for North Carolina records, I typed *abstract* into the Title box and *north carolina* into the Keyword(s) box, resulting in eight hits (**A**). I selected "Abstract of North Carolina Wills, 1663–1760" and searched for John Snow.

Now here's the tricky part: If I didn't check the Exact box for both John and Snow, the search returned pages that had the word *john* and the word *snow* but not necessarily in the same name. When I checked Exact, I found five results. One of them (**B**) was of a family member. The information abstracted only the pertinent information.

One last point about this particular collection: Although you can use the collection's search box, you'll see that you can read through the entire book on the right side of the page. I suggest reading at least the introduction when using this or any collection that allows browsing a book. That's because introductions typically give additional information about the resource; in this case, you'll find an explanation of the use of a person's mark instead of a signature, the misleading use of mother-in-law and father-in-law, and information about whether original spelling was preserved.

A   ❸

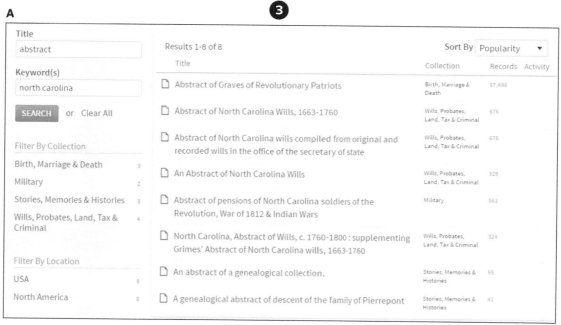

B

PORTOBWIN, PETER.

August 23, 1729. June 10, 1730. *Sons:* JOSEPH and SAMUEL. *Sons-in-law:* JOHN SNOW, FRANCIS DESHUNG. *Witnesses:* JOHN ARTER, THOMAS HUTCHINGS, ANTHONY MARCK. Proven before RICHARD EVERARD.

➤ Use the general search form only when you're just starting a search and have little information or when you've exhausted all other search strategies.

➤ Search specific categories of records using the other search forms under the Search tab when you have a clear search goal and a good idea of where to find the record.

➤ Identify and select specific collections (or categories of collections) using the Card Catalog. Use the Card Catalog's filters to discover collections with the most probable chances for success.

➤ Determine the most appropriate time period using the Card Catalog's decade filter. This can be especially useful when two people have the same name and live in the same place, but were alive during different times.

➤ Follow Ancestry.com's suggested collections. Oftentimes, you've never considered (or have even heard of) the records that Ancestry.com suggests for your research, but these can open up new areas of study. Click the Show More link at the bottom of the initial list to expand the list of suggestions.

ANCESTOR INFORMATION CHEAT SHEET

Using this worksheet, note important search details and parameters about one relative to save time when filling out Ancestry.com search forms.

WORKSHEET FOR: _____

Names to search

Consider all possible spellings, transcription errors, etc.—you never know how your ancestor will show up in an index.

Ancestor's First Name		**Variations**	
Ancestor's Middle Name		**Variations**	
Ancestor's Last Name		**Variations**	
Nicknames and Other Variants			

Vital statistics

When searching online, try date ranges (such as +/- 1–5 years), as not all records include precise or accurate dates. Don't include dates that would eliminate certain records you're seeking: Death dates won't appear on a marriage record, for example.

Birth date		**Birthplace (city, county, state)**	
Marriage date		**Marriage place (city, county, state)**	
Death date		**Death place (city, county, state)**	

Residences

If you don't get results when searching narrowly (city or county), expand to a wider area (state or country).

Lived in		**Years**	
Lived in		**Years**	
Lived in		**Years**	
Lived in		**Years**	

Family members

Other relatives named on a record can help you distinguish your ancestor from others of the same name in the same place.

Spouse's name		**Birth date**	
Spouse's name		**Birth date**	
Father's name		**Birth date**	
Mother's name		**Birth date**	
Child's name		**Birth date**	
Child's name		**Birth date**	
Child's name		**Birth date**	
Child's name		**Birth date**	

ONLINE SEARCH TRACKER: ANCESTRY.COM SEARCH FORMS

To avoid duplicating work, use this worksheet to track your searches on Ancestry.com and their results. You can download a version of this worksheet online at <ftu.familytreemagazine.com/unofficial-ancestry-workbook>.

	Search #1	Search #2	Search #3
Collection name and URL			
Name (First, middle, last)			
Birth/death information (Birth year and place, death year and place)			
Lived in			
Immigration information (Arrival year, port, origin, nationality, ship)			
Marriage information (Year, spouse)			
Family members (Mother, father, siblings, children)			
Keywords			
Results			

ONLINE SEARCH TRACKER: ANCESTRY.COM CARD CATALOG

To streamline your efforts, use this worksheet to track your searches for Ancestry.com collections in the Card Catalog. You can download a version of this worksheet online at <ftu.familytreemagazine.com/unofficial-ancestry-workbook>.

Category searched	Title(s)	Keyword(s)	Filter(s)	Results	Notes

QUICK GUIDE: ANCESTRY.COM CATEGORIES AND SUBCATEGORIES

Use this quick guide to identify potential categories and subcategories worth searching in the Ancestry.com Card Catalog.

Census & Voter Lists
(Organized by century and decade)

Birth, Marriage & Death
- Birth, Baptism & Christening
- Marriage & Divorce
- Death, Burial, Cemetery & Obituaries

Military
- Draft, Enlistment and Service
- Casualties
- Soldier, Veteran & Prisoner Rolls & Lists
- Pension Records
- Histories
- Awards & Decorations of Honor
- News
- Disciplinary Actions
- Photos

Immigration & Travel
- Passenger Lists
- Crew Lists
- Border Crossings & Passports
- Citizenship & Naturalization Records
- Immigration & Emigration Books
- Ship Pictures & Descriptions

Newspapers & Publications
- Newspapers
- Periodicals & Magazines

Pictures

Stories, Memories & Histories
- Family Histories, Journals & Biographies
- Oral Histories & Interviews
- Social & Place Histories
- Society & Organization Histories
- Military Histories
- Royalty, Nobility & Heraldry

Maps, Atlases & Gazetteers
- Maps & Atlases
- Gazetteers

Schools, Directories & Church Histories
- City & Area Directories
- Professional & Organizational Directories
- Church Histories & Records
- School Lists & Yearbooks
- Telephone Directories

Wills, Probates, Land, Tax & Criminal
- Land Records
- Tax Lists
- Court, Governmental & Criminal Records
- Wills & Probates, Estates & Guardian Records
- Bank & Insurance Records

Reference, Dictionaries & Almanacs
- General Reference Materials
- Research Guides & Finding Aids
- Dictionaries & Encyclopedias
- Almanacs, Country Studies & Gazetteers

Family Trees

2

CENSUS RECORDS

I've always considered census records to be the backbone of genealogy research. It's the one type of record that places a family unit or an individual in a specific time at a specific place. For example, census records provide clues and valuable details about where and how your ancestors lived (e.g., street addresses, names of neighbors). Although other records like marriages tell us where and when we can find an individual, census records paint a full picture and allow us to identify areas of further research.

However, early census records can be a challenge, as only heads of household were listed by name; all other occupants were simply noted by an age bracket. It wasn't until 1850 (the sixth federal census) that everyone in a dwelling was named. (Note that slaves, then considered property, were not included. Authorities conducted separate schedules in 1850 and 1860 to account for slaves.)

While the questions asked on a census vary from decade to decade, each is filled with questions that open more and more doors of research. For example, in 1850, we can find place of birth, occupation, and value of the person's real estate. By 1870, questions about foreign-born parents were added, along with questions that asked respondents to differentiate the value of their personal estate from the value of their real estate. The 1880 census added a column for illness at the time of the enumerator's visit, and we're given a year the person immigrated to the United States in the 1900 census. Among these questions, the one that really pops out for me is why the 1880 census included a question about illness. Was it because diphtheria was running rampant during that time period? This points to more research that can be done.

Although most genealogy research is done via the US federal censuses from 1790 through 1940, other censuses taken include state censuses, slave schedules, agricultural censuses and other non-population schedules (1850–1880). Let's take a look at what's available on Ancestry.com.

FEDERAL CENSUSES

Why does the United States conduct a nationwide census every ten years? The Constitution specifies that the number of seats in the House of Representatives is distributed proportionally among the states based on population counts in the census. If we weren't counted, there would be no way of fairly assigning seats in the House.

But the US census has another, more immediate use for genealogists. US federal census records are some of the few standard records to be taken at regular intervals, allowing you to follow an individual or family line through decades with relative ease.

From 1790 through 1840, the federal census named only the head of household; other family members were enumerated only by age, gender, and free or slave status. Over time, the age categories themselves changed from only two age groups for free white males in 1790 to twelve for free whites and six for slaves and free colored persons in 1840. This lack of names presents a thorny problem for genealogists, as it requires us to evaluate the likelihood that a person of interest in

Using Pre-1850 Federal Censuses

Because federal censuses before 1850 have less information than later enumerations, we have to take some extra steps when working with them. Check out these five quick steps to using pre-1850 federal censuses.

1. Starting with the 1850 census, make a list of everyone in the household, their estimated ages in 1850, and their estimated dates of birth.

2. Subtract ten years from each person's age and see if you can find a potential match for this family in the 1840 census, and backward. For example, the 1850 census tells you that you know your family has a father (age forty-five), a mother (age forty-four), a son (age seventeen), and a daughter (age fifteen). Next, look in the 1840 census for a family with the same name: head-of-household father (age thirty-five), mother (age thirty-four), boy (age seven), and girl (age five). But what if you find two more children in the 1840 census than appear on the 1850 census? Depending on age, it's possible the children either were out of the home or deceased by the 1850 census. If, over the course of years the ages seem to correlate, you may have found the right family. If a young child in 1840 is gone from the 1850 census,

this presents another clue: Start searching death records.

3. As you evaluate several census years, narrow down ages and create a chart of possible birth years for family members. Ancestry.com will help with this, as indexed entries for each family will have an estimated birth year. Once you have potential birth years, you can begin searching in other types of records, such as marriage, birth, and land.

4. Try to determine an approximate date of death. Let's say the head of household was alive in 1800, but by 1810 his wife is listed as a widow (Wd.). Now you know that he died sometime between the 1800 and the 1810 census.

5. As you work your way back through various federal censuses, don't forget to search state census records.

The reality is, evaluating families via pre-1850 censuses takes a lot of guesswork, some of which won't be correct. But your chance of success will increase by using worksheets and carefully evaluating the facts you have.

Don't forget to check Ancestry.com's own resource on creating pre-1850 cheat sheets <www.ancestry.com/cs/learning/20100608Pre1850Census>.

---

the ten-year-old category in 1810 is the same person in the twenty-year-old category in 1820.

While this group of 1790–1840 censuses won't help you quickly skip back through generations like 1850 and beyond, the resources can help you gain an understanding of the basic structure of the household. Of course, you probably won't know if the three girls in an age group were children, stepchildren, or even nieces, but it can help as you move from census to census to try to pinpoint who was who—not an easy task. See the Using Pre-1850 Federal Censuses sidebar for strategies utilizing these resources.

Ancestry.com hosts digitized images of every federal census from 1790 through 1940. Each federal census contains slightly different questions; see the US Federal Census Questions At a Glance worksheet at the end of the chapter, and see appendix C for census abstract forms. Note that the 1890 census is largely missing due to a fire and resulting water damage, so you'll have to turn to census substitutes (such as the 1890 Veterans Schedule and Ancestry.com's 1890 census substitute collection; see Exercise #2). Because

of a seventy-two-year privacy policy, the 1950 census won't be released until 2022.

SLAVE SCHEDULES

In 1850 and 1860, the United States conducted a special schedule to determine how many slaves were in the country, and both of these schedules are searchable at Ancestry.com. Unlike US citizens in the federal census, slaves were not enumerated by name. Rather, they were logged by number and organized by the name of the slaveowner (image **A**). On this census, you'll find: the name and residence of the owner; the number of slaves; the slaves' age, sex, and color; and whether the slave was a fugitive or had been released from slavery. In addition, the 1860 census included a question regarding the number of slave houses on the property.

Slave schedules can be tricky to use, so proceed with caution. In preparing the exercises for this chapter, I thought I would try to track down someone using a slave schedule, but this particular problem turned out to be too tough. I have very little information on a family with slave roots—my only solid lead is a birth date of 1884 for Fannie Davis, born in Pine Bluff, Arkansas. Her parents are listed as Stephen Davis and Mymie Tobler. As slave schedules typically don't include the name of the slave, this would force me to track down a slave owner in (possibly) Arkansas with the surname of Davis or Tobler. I don't have any dates of birth, ages, or place of residence. In searching the 1860 slave schedule for Stephen Davis in Arkansas, Ancestry.com returned several thousand results, many in Mississippi. Without a few more details, I have no way of knowing if any of these are the right person.

For best results, gather as much information as possible before delving into slave schedules. Researching them can be overwhelming without dates, names, and places.

STATE CENSUSES

State censuses were often taken in the years between the federal census, and Ancestry.com has several of them <www.ancestry.com/cs/learning/state-census-collections>. Some state censuses were taken as early as the late 1700s and as late as 1945. According to the Census Bureau, "State censuses often can serve as substitutes for some of the missing federal census records—most notably the 1790, 1800, 1810, and 1890 censuses. Many state censuses also asked different questions than the federal census, thus recording information that cannot be found elsewhere in the federal schedules." In other words, state censuses can help you fill in gaps left by federal census records or give more color about what your ancestors' lives were like—and what your ancestors had been up to since the latest federal census.

NON-POPULATION SCHEDULES

Governments also collected "non-population" schedules, so named because they dealt with agriculture and manufacturing. If you have an ancestor listed in these records (image **B**), you can discover the value of his farm, the number of various livestock (e.g., horses, mules, cows), and the number of bushels of agricultural product (e.g., wheat, rye, corn, oats, rice, tobacco).

Ancestry.com has a single, massive collection of non-population schedules: "Selected U.S. Federal Census Non-Population Schedules, 1850–1880." These records are from twenty-one states, including agriculture infor-

A

Slave schedules can give information about your slave ancestors, who wouldn't have been enumerated by name in the federal census.

B

Non-population schedules can provide information about your ancestors, such as the number of livestock they owned.

mation, industry/manufacturers information, social statistics, and supplemental census data.

MORTALITY SCHEDULES

These schedules record deaths in the year preceding the federal census, allowing you to learn a little more about ancestors who may not have lived to see the most recent census. (Many federal censuses were officially taken on June 1, so the "preceding year" means the twelve preceding months, beginning on June 1 of the previous year.) These schedules contain

C

Name:	Ida Hendrickson
Gender:	Female
Marital Status:	Widowed
Estimated birth year:	abt 1774
Birth Place:	New York, USA
Age:	86
Death Date:	Mar 1860
Cause of Death:	Old Age
Census Year:	1860
Census Place:	Hamilton, Mercer, New Jersey, USA
LINE:	21

Add alternate information

Report issue

SAVE ∨   Cancel

Mortality schedules give information about relatives who died within a year of a federal census, potentially helping you find ancestors "missing" from the census.

What Was the Cause of Death?

The mortality schedules of 1850 and 1860 represent an archive of the nation's health. When using the "U.S., Federal Census Mortality Schedules Index, 1850–1880," search by county instead of by name. I searched the collection for *1860 Bronx County, New York*, which brought in more than thirteen hundred hits. Skimming the results reveal many causes of death, including accidental deaths from drowning and the most common cause of death, consumption (known today as tuberculosis).

Compare the Bronx County, New York, deaths with those of 1850 San Francisco County, California. Interestingly, Gold Rush miners in San Francisco County were hit harder by cholera, diarrhea, and violence (including shooting, stabbing, and hanging), while Bronx County residents were far more likely to die from consumption. Note: If you see "diarrhea" as a cause of death while many people nearby were listed as dying of cholera, it's probable the actual cause of death for that person was also cholera; diarrhea was a common symptom of cholera.

If you can't find your family listed in the mortality schedules, take the time to track down the statistics from where they lived to learn about the diseases they faced. Want to save some time in your disease research? Don't bother searching Google for *1850 treatment for cholera* or *nineteenth-century treatment of scarlet fever*; unfortunately for our ancestors, those treatments didn't exist.

information on the name, age, and sex of the deceased, as well as the individual's place and month of birth, cause of death, and profession (image **C**). In addition, the people you find in this index will be linked to the census image on which they appear.

As with non-population schedules, Ancestry.com has a single collection in this category: "U.S. Federal Census Mortality Schedules, 1850–1885." This collection includes the federal mortality schedule as well as mortality schedules from three state censuses (Colorado, Florida, and Nebraska).

1890 VETERANS SCHEDULE

This 1890 census was taken to enumerate Civil War Union Veterans and their widows, and it's available on Ancestry.com. Veterans schedules included military service years, unit, and dates of enlistment and discharge, as well as any physical ailments relating to military service (image **D**). In some areas, Confederate soldiers were also listed. Although the veterans schedule does not list everyone living in the household, it will include enough information about the veteran to (hopefully) find him on earlier and later federal censuses—and the census can be a nice substitute for the destroyed 1890 federal US census. See chapter 4 for more information on military records.

VOTER REGISTRATIONS

My guess is that not many people are aware of the category of census-type information in voter registration records. Here, you can possibly find registrants' ages, residences, and occupations. However, some, like those in the California collection (image **E**), include items like date and place of naturalization. Ancestry.com only has a handful of collections, covering data from California; Texas; Illinois (Chicago); Georgia (Savannah); Kansas; Missouri; Alabama; and Arizona.

D

The 1890 veterans schedule records the military service years, dates of enlistment and discharge, unit, and more for Civil War (Union) soldiers.

E

Voter registrations, if you can find them, can provide your ancestor's age, residence, occupation, and even date and place of naturalization.

RESEARCH GOAL: *Find Herschel B. Hendrickson in the 1940 census.*

STEP ❶ Find the 1940 census collection.

Choose Search from the main (top) menu, then Census & Voter Lists from the drop-down menu. On the right side of the page, select "1940 United States Federal Census" under Featured data collections (**A**).

If this census is not among your choices (depending on when you're using this workbook, you may have different selections), choose Narrow by Category, also on the right side of the page (**B**). Select U.S. Federal Census Collection, then on the next page select the 1940 census.

STEP ❷ Fill in the basic information.

In this instance, I added only name, year and place of birth, and "lived in." I could have added more information, but I wanted to see if this would suffice.

STEP ❸ Review your results.

Fortunately, the first result was exactly the person I was searching for. Do you notice the pencil icon? That means someone has edited the information on this census. While the enumerator only entered the name as *HB*, another Ancestry.com user noted that the name was Herschel Byron.

A ❶

> ### Featured data collections
>
> 1940 United States Federal Census [FREE]
>
> Australia, Electoral Rolls, 1903-1980 [UPDATED]
>
> U.S., Indian Census Rolls, 1885-1940
>
> [VIEW ALL IN CARD CATALOG]

B

> ### Narrow by Category
>
> U.S. Federal Census Collection
>
> U.K. Census Collection
>
> Canadian Census Collection, 1851-1916
>
> 1700s Censuses
>
> 1800s Censuses
>
> 1900s Censuses

❷

❸

EXERCISE ② Using 1890 Census Substitutes

RESEARCH GOAL: *Find any Missouri Faulkenberrys in an 1890 census substitute.*

STEP ❶ Find the appropriate substitute.

For this search, I'll use Ancestry.com's "1890 Census Substitute," a collection of records that fill in some of the gaps left by the 1890 census' destruction that includes surviving 1890-census fragments, plus multiple state censuses and city directories. You can find the collection here <search.ancestry.com/search/group/1890census>.

STEP ❷ Enter your search terms.

I typed *Faulkenberry* in the Last Name box and *Jackson County, Missouri* in the Lived In box. This resulted in close to three thousand hits—way too many to investigate.

STEP ❸ Narrow your results.

I clicked Edit search and changed Jackson County to Exact to this place. This search was far better—only fourteen results, each of them in a city directory and none in a state census or the veterans schedule. Unfortunately, none of the results were my ancestors. However, I went to both the 1880 and the 1900 censuses and found the family members I was looking for.

❶

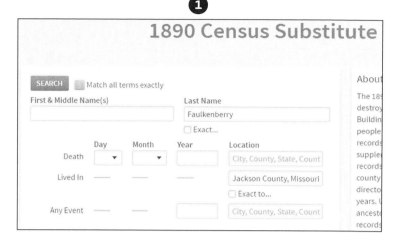

❷

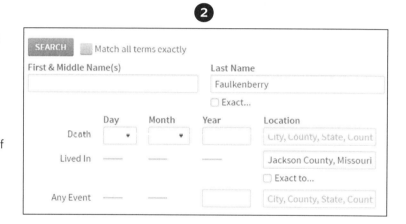

❸

EXERCISE ③ Finding Information in a Special Schedule

RESEARCH GOAL: *Find information in a mortality schedule about any of my Cave ancestors in Missouri.*

STEP ❶ Find your collection.

Go to the Card Catalog and filter for Census & Voter Lists. Then type *mortality* in the Keyword(s) box. Of the five resultant collections, I selected "Missouri Mortality Records, 1850 and 1860."

STEP ❷ Enter your search terms.

Because I didn't know which, if any, Cave family members would be on the schedule, I only entered the surname in the search box and left all other search boxes empty.

❶

Title	Collection	Records	Activity
Results 1-5 of 5		Sort By Popularity ▾	
Search entire "Census & Voter Lists" Category			
U.S. Federal Census Mortality Schedules, 1850-1885	Census & Voter Lists	1,607,736	
U.S., Federal Census Mortality Schedules Index, 1850-1880	Census & Voter Lists	492,925	
New York, U.S. Census Mortality Schedules, 1850-1880	Census & Voter Lists	263,880	
Missouri Mortality Records, 1850 and 1860	Census & Voter Lists	2,060	
Montgomery County, New York mortality schedules	Census & Voter Lists	62	

❷

SEARCH ☐ Match all terms exactly

First & Middle Name(s)

Last Name
cave
☐ Exact...

Year Location

Any Event [ ] City, County, State, Country ▾

Keyword

e.g. pilot or "Flying Tigers" ⌄

SEARCH Clear search

STEP ❸ Review your results.

The search resulted in two hits for surname Cave on this Missouri Mortality Schedule. I'm not sure Nancy Cave is one of my family members, but the birthplace of Virginia caught my eye since I know many of the Cave family originated in the Old Dominion. More research is needed.

STEP ❹ Search more broadly.

I could stop here, but I wanted to cast a wider net. I returned to the original five Mortality Schedule collections and selected "U.S. Federal Census Mortality Schedules, 1850–1885." But when I noticed Missouri was not a part of this collection, I selected "U.S., Federal Census Mortality Schedules Index, 1850–1880." According to the information about the collection, the only year Missouri is included is 1860.

Again, I only entered the surname and the location (*Missouri*) but selected Exact to this place (**A**), as I knew from past searches that *Cave* as a search parameter alone would return too many results.

There were two results, neither of which belonged to my family (**B**). But it's worthwhile noting that although I selected Missouri as Exact, an Iowa death was one of the results. This is because Andrew Cave, who died in Iowa, was born in Missouri.

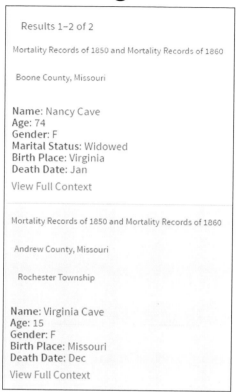

❸

Results 1–2 of 2

Mortality Records of 1850 and Mortality Records of 1860

Boone County, Missouri

Name: Nancy Cave
Age: 74
Gender: F
Marital Status: Widowed
Birth Place: Virginia
Death Date: Jan

View Full Context

Mortality Records of 1850 and Mortality Records of 1860

Andrew County, Missouri

Rochester Township

Name: Virginia Cave
Age: 15
Gender: F
Birth Place: Missouri
Death Date: Dec

View Full Context

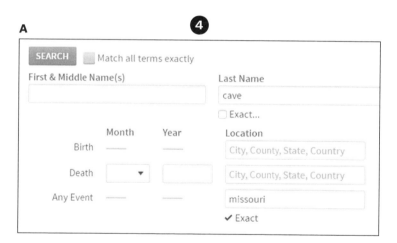

A

❹

SEARCH ☐ Match all terms exactly

First & Middle Name(s)

Last Name

cave

☐ Exact...

	Month	Year	Location
Birth	⎯	⎯	City, County, State, Country
Death	▼		City, County, State, Country
Any Event	⎯	⎯	missouri

✔ Exact

B

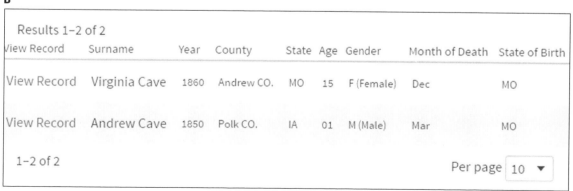

Results 1–2 of 2

View Record	Surname	Year	County	State	Age	Gender	Month of Death	State of Birth
View Record	Virginia Cave	1860	Andrew CO.	MO	15	F (Female)	Dec	MO
View Record	Andrew Cave	1850	Polk CO.	IA	01	M (Male)	Mar	MO

1–2 of 2

Per page 10 ▼

➤ Estimate your ancestor's date of birth using the age given on the census. You can use age estimates from census to census to separate two people with the same name. In a similar way, the 1900 and 1910 censuses asked for the number of years the person was married, allowing you to count backwards to your ancestor's marriage date.

➤ Print off a blank census form for each year so you'll have a handy reference for the questions asked on each census. The US Federal Census Questions At a Glance worksheet provides a list, and you can find templates for each federal census in appendix C.

➤ Look for clues about your ancestor's life before that year's census. Questions in individual censuses can reap rewarding (and sometimes unique) information about your ancestors. For example, the 1840 census asked for the ages of Revolutionary War pensioners.

➤ Begin your census search widely—for example, start with name and state, then narrow to county.

➤ Identify life events that happened during a census year. For example, the 1870 and 1880 censuses asked for month of birth if the person was born "within the year," which will help you nail down a date of birth for children born around the census. Similarly, the 1850 to 1880 censuses hold clues about date of marriage, as they asked if a person was married within the year.

➤ Be aware of changing county boundary lines. Based on how lines shifted over the years, you may be looking for an ancestor in the wrong county.

➤ Discover all the children born to an ancestor, even those who were no longer living at the time of the census. The 1900 and 1910 show the number of children born to the woman as well as the number of children still living.

➤ Look for clues about your ancestor's immigration and naturalization in the census record. (See chapter 5.)

➤ Don't assume your ancestor was skipped during an enumeration. Look for alternate surname spellings, first name shown as initials (e.g., *D.J.* instead of *Donald J*), or location in a neighboring county. I have found Hendrickson ancestors on various census records with spellings of: *Hendrixson*, *Hendrixon*, *Hendricks*, and *Hendrisson*.

➤ Don't stop your search with the federal census; see if your ancestors can be found in statewide census records.

➤ Use census records to paint a picture of your family's financial status. Census records can include value of property, whether a home is rented or owned, or, in the case of an agricultural schedule, the numbers of livestock and crops.

Each federal census' coverage was different. Use this at-a-glance chart to determine which questions were asked in which censuses. See appendix C for abstract templates to use while researching and recording federal census records.

Category	Question	1790	1800	1810	1820	1830	1840	1850	1860	1870	1880	1890	1900	1910	1920	1930	1940
Names	Head of household's name	•	•	•	•	•	•	•	•	•	•	•	•	•	•	•	•
Names	All household members' names (except slaves)							•	•	•	•	•	•	•	•	•	•
Birth information	Age ranges of free white males	•	•	•	•	•	•										
Birth information	Age ranges of free white females		•	•	•	•	•										
Birth information	Ages of all household members							•	•	•	•		•	•	•	•	•
Birth information	Birthplace							•	•	•	•	•	•	•	•	•	•
Birth information	Month and year of birth												•				
Parents	Foreign-born parents									•							
Parents	Parents' birthplaces										•	•	•	•	•	•	
Parents	Mother tongue													•	•	•	•
Parents	Parents' mother tongues													•	•		
Marriage	Married in the census year							•	•	•	•		•				
Marriage	Marital status										•		•	•	•	•	•
Marriage	Years married												•	•			
Marriage	Age at first marriage															•	
Immigration and citizenship	Number of aliens/non-naturalized residents				•	•	•										
Immigration and citizenship	Year of immigration												•	•	•	•	
Immigration and citizenship	Years in the United States												•	•			
Immigration and citizenship	Naturalization status											•	•	•	•	•	•
Other	Number of free colored				•	•	•										
Other	Relationship to head of household										•		•	•	•	•	•
Other	Veteran status											•		•		•	•
Other	Number of children mothered (living and total)											•	•	•			

US CENSUS RECORDS CHECKLIST

Ancestor's name	
Ancestor's maiden name (if female)	
Residence/location(s)	
Date of birth	
Birthplace	
Mother's name	
Mother's date of birth	
Mother's birthplace	
Father's name	
Father's date of birth	
Father's birthplace	
Other member(s) of household	

Look for your ancestor in all US censuses taken during his or her lifetime. Put a check mark next to the year after you've found his or her census listing, and save a copy for your records. Cross off any censuses that occurred before your ancestor was born or after he or she died.

Federal censuses

☐ 1790   ☐ 1830   ☐ 1870   ☐ 1910

☐ 1800   ☐ 1840   ☐ 1880   ☐ 1920

☐ 1810   ☐ 1850   ☐ 1890   ☐ 1930

☐ 1820   ☐ 1860   ☐ 1900   ☐ 1940

State/Territorial censuses

Research statewide censuses for your ancestor's state, and record information about them below.

State name: _____

State census dates to check:

☐ _____   ☐ _____

☐ _____   ☐ _____

☐ _____   ☐ _____

Special censuses on Ancestry.com

If you think your ancestor might be in a special census, search those collections on Ancestry.com. Put a check in the box next to the census once you've searched it.

☐ U.S. Federal Census Mortality Schedule, 1850–1885

☐ 1850 U.S. Federal Census—Slave Schedules

☐ 1860 U.S. Federal Census—Slave Schedules

☐ 1930 Census of Merchant Seamen

☐ _____

☐ _____

☐ _____

Adapted from Unofficial Guide to FamilySearch.org. *Copyright © 2015 Dana McCullough*

BIRTH, MARRIAGE, AND DEATH RECORDS

I f census records are number one on the genealogy hit parade, birth, marriage, and death records run a close second. That's because they are the *official* records that document the major events of a person's life.

For genealogists, vital records are critical in proving both relationships and events. For example, family legend may place a marriage in Virginia when, in fact, vital records prove it was in South Carolina. Any time we can find documentation of an event (especially vital events that occurred at pivotal moments in our ancestors' lives), we get closer to cracking the family tree code.

While census records top the charts because of their regularity (federal censuses have been required every ten years since 1790), birth, marriage, and death records were governed by far less stringent regulations. Some records were kept by towns as soon as they were founded, while churches kept others (particularly marriage records). However, on a state level, these "vital records" weren't typically mandated until the early twentieth century.

This means that, in your genealogy research, you'll need to delve into church and civil records at a local level, particularly when researching pre-twentieth century records. Town records—most often found in early New England and kept from the town's beginning onward—are where you can find vital records along with other documents such as tax records, surveys, and burials.

Ancestry.com has a robust collection of vital records, with more than one thousand US collections and more than seven hundred from Europe. The broad category of Birth, Marriage & Death records on Ancestry.com is broken down into three main subcategories:

1. Birth, Baptism & Christening
2. Marriage & Divorce
3. Death, Burial, Cemetery & Obituaries

Let's see what each contains and how to get the most from your vital records research.

BIRTH, BAPTISM & CHRISTENING

As you might imagine, these records all pertain to the beginning of a life. The earliest of these records, beginning in the 1600s, center around New England. Some are based on Quaker meeting records, while others are based on town records, wills, churches, and family Bible records.

This collection of birth-related vital records contains more than sixteen hundred collections. One of these, "Names in Stone," is an amazing collection of seventy-five thousand tombstone inscriptions from Frederick County, Maryland. It won't necessarily give you much more than a birth date, but sometimes that's all it takes to push your research one step further back in time.

When searching early town or church records, you'll probably find the name of the child and his or her parents, plus a birth date. The collections often include information about how records are organized or presented, telling you how to "decode" what you're seeing; be sure to read this before you dive into the records. For example, image **A** shows an entry from

A

Campbell Thomas 16 July 1853
Pat Ellen Not Listed 10 July
Jas Mc Keon & Mary Mc Keon

Reading about a collection's records can help you decipher them. For example, I know this entry is for "Thomas Campbell," rather than "Campbell Thomas," because the source's entries are organized alphabetically by last name.

"Brooklyn, New York, St. Paul's Catholic Church Baptism Records, 1837–1900," which gives the child's name (Thomas Campbell), the date of baptism (16 July 1853), the child's date of birth (10 July), the names of the child's parents (Pat and Ellen [Thomas]), and the name of the child's godparents (James and Mary Mc Keon).

The information found on birth records will almost always include the child's name, sex, date and place of birth, and the names of the parents. Baptism and christening records will vary depending on the practices of the church or religion.

MARRIAGE & DIVORCE

Interestingly, marriages were documented very early—oftentimes earlier than births or deaths. With more than thirteen hundred US collections in this collection, you can access both very early and fairly recent records. Although privacy laws will prohibit you from viewing more current records, you'll actually be able to find indexes of US marriages up into the twenty-first century. For example, Washington (state) has records dating to 2004 while Texas' records stretch to 2011.

Marriage records typically include the name of the bride and groom, their ages, the date and place of the wedding, and the names of witnesses and officiant. Some records will also indicate that the bride is at least eighteen years of age.

Divorce records are not as easy to find, with only about twenty-seven US collections on Ancestry.com containing the word *divorce* in their title. The earliest of these records are from the twentieth century, with some exceptions such as Maine (which has divorce records dating from 1798).

Divorce indexes, like the "Texas Divorce Index," give only scant information, as you can see in image **B**. Some earlier records have a little more information like the ones from the "New Hampshire, Marriage and Divorce Records, 1659–1947." Here, a divorce record (image **C**) can also contain the date and place of marriage as well as the name of the person who performed the marriage ceremony.

DEATH, BURIAL, CEMETERY & OBITUARIES

The broadest of the three collections with more than eighteen hundred collections, the Death, Burial, Cemetery & Obituaries category is where you'll find a little bit of everything, from death indexes and death certificates to town records, the Social Security Death Index, obituaries, funeral home records, and veteran death index cards.

B

Name:	Dorothy W Aahon
Estimated birth year:	abt 1920
Age:	50
Spouse's Name:	Leon T Aahon
Spouse's Age:	49
Marriage Date:	16 Aug 1963
Number of Children:	0
Divorce Date:	15 Oct 1970
Divorce Place:	Bexar, Texas, USA

Divorce indexes provide limited (but still important) information.

C

Some divorce records provide such detail as the name of the person who performed the original marriage ceremony.

D

DEPARTMENT OF COMMERCE
BUREAU OF THE CENSUS

THE STATE BOARD OF HEALTH OF MISSOURI
STANDARD CERTIFICATE OF DEATH

State File No. **28927**

FILED SEP 27 1948 42
Registration District No. 42

Primary Registration District No. 1000

Registrar's No. 993

1. PLACE OF DEATH:
(a) County Buchanan
(b) City or town St. Joseph
(If outside city or town limits, write "RURAL" and name of township)
(c) Name of hospital or institution:
General Hospital
(If not in hospital or institution, write street number or location)
(d) Length of stay: In hospital or institution 5 days
In this community 21 years.
(Specify whether years, months or days)

2. USUAL RESIDENCE OF DECEASED:
(a) State Missouri (b) County Buchanan
(c) City or town St. Joseph
(If outside city or town limits, write "RURAL.")
(d) Street No. 1904 S. 11th Street
(If rural, give location)
(e) Citizen of foreign country? No.
(Yes or No)
If yes, name country

MEDICAL CERTIFICATION

3. (a) PRINT FULL NAME: Herschel Byron Hendrickson

3. (b) If veteran, name war None
3. (c) Social Security No. Unknown

4. Sex Male
5. Color or race White
6. (a) Single, widowed, married, divorced Married
6. (b) Name of husband or wife Bessie Hendrickson
6. (c) Age of husband or wife if alive 57 years
7. Birth date of deceased August 18 1888
(Month) (Day) (Year)

8. AGE: Years 60 Months 0 Days 27 If less than one day hr. min.

9. Birthplace Jackson County Missouri
(City, town, or county) (State or foreign country)
10. Usual occupation Owner
11. Industry or business Heating Contractor

FATHER
12. Name James Hendrickson
13. Birthplace Unknown Indiana
(City, town, or county) (State or foreign country)

MOTHER
14. Maiden name Ella Snow
15. Birthplace Unknown Missouri
(City, town, or county) (State or foreign country)

16. (a) Informant Mrs. Bessie Hendrickson
(b) Address 1904 S. 11th St., St. Joseph, Mo.
17. (a) Removal (b) Date thereof Sept. 17, 1948
(Burial, cremation, or removal) (Month) (Day) (Year)
(c) Place: burial or cremation John Jack, Missouri.
18. (a) Signature of funeral director Walter Meierhoffer
(b) Address 1946 Colhoun St., St. Joseph, Mo.
19. (a) 9-20-48 (b) E. C. Jenkins
(Date received local registrar) (Registrar's signature)

20. DATE OF DEATH: Month September year 1948 hour 2 minute 30 A. M. 15th

21. I hereby certify that I attended the deceased from Dec 24th 1946 to Sept 14th 1948 that I last saw him alive on Sept 14th 1948 and that death occurred on the date and hour stated above.

Immediate cause of death Hypostatic Pneumonia — Duration 6 hrs
Due to myocarditis — 2 yrs
Due to

Other conditions Enlarged liver
(Include pregnancy within 3 months of death)

Major findings:
Of operations
Of autopsy 938

PHYSICIAN
Underline the cause to which death should be charged statistically.

22. If death was due to external causes, fill in the following:
(a) Accident, suicide, or homicide (specify)
(b) Date of occurrence
(c) Where did injury occur? (City or town) (County) (State)
(d) Did injury occur in or about home, on farm, in industrial place, in public place?
(Specify type of place)
While at work (e) Means of injury

23. Signature John Hartrock D.O.
Address 224 Logan Bldg. Date signed 9-15-48
St. Joseph, Mo.

(Licensed Embalmer's Statement on Reverse Side)

Death certificates include a wealth of information about the deceased and his family.

In general, death records (particularly death certificates; see image **D**) can open up new lines of research, primarily because they can contain the name of the person's parents (including the mother's maiden name) as well as where the parents and the decedent were born. They might also show age, occupation, name of attending physician, cause of death, length of illness, address, the name of the informant, and place of burial. Not all records contain all of these things, but many do.

The most important thing to remember is that the person giving the information (informant) may not know the answers to all of the questions or may be too upset to give correct answers, so it's possible information such as the mother's maiden name or place of birth of the parents is incorrect. As you'll see in one of our exercises later in this chapter, it's always a good idea to confirm information in death records by consulting other sources. See appendix B for a list of sources to consult when looking for birth, marriage, and death information.

Among the millions of death records held by Ancestry.com is a gem for New England researchers, "The New England Historical & Genealogical Register, 1847–2011." These records, taken from this quarterly publication, can include a whole host of

E

8. OCCUPATION OF DECEASED	
(a) Trade, profession, or particular kind of work	*Retired*
(b) General nature of industry, business or establishment in which employed (or employer)	
(c) Name of employer	

9. BIRTHPLACE (city or town)	*England*
(State or Country)	

PARENTS

10. NAME OF FATHER	*Jos. Brooks*
11. BIRTHPLACE OF FATHER (city or town) .... (State or Country)	
MAIDEN 12. NAME OF MOTHER	*Jennie James*
13. BIRTHPLACE OF MOTHER (city or town) (State or Country)	*England*

Death certificates provide information, not just about the decedent, but also about his parents.

genealogical information. However, if you can't find your family here, be sure to read the description of the collection, as it includes tips for finding people who may not show up in your initial search.

Although finding ancestors in an index or register is a great starting place, you'll have even more clues to research if you're fortunate enough to find their death certificate. For example, as you can see in image **E**, the decedent's parents are both named (including maiden name) along with their place of birth. Obituaries can also provide useful information (image **F**).

You can also find helpful information in funeral home records, although these records are scant on Ancestry.com. One collection of San Francisco-area funeral home records contains a brief index, shown in image **G**. In addition, you can sometimes find a funeral home card that lists name, age, occupation, place of birth, place of death (address), itemized costs for funeral expenses, and name of the deceased's chosen casket—probably more information than most of us want to know!

F

KOPPIT
Julius A. Koppit, age 79, of 476 Garland, Romeoville, Sept. 17, 1975, husband of the late Martha (Barbott); father of Mrs. Levi (Joan) Fox of Romeoville, Mrs. Ronald (Hazel) Mahnke of Alsip, Ill., William and Elmer of Romeoville; grandfather of 11. Services at the Goodale Funeral Home, 912 S. Hamilton St., Lockport, Friday, Sept. 19, at 10:30 a.m. Interment Concordia, Forest Park. Visitation 2 to 4 and 7 to 9 p.m. Thursday. Memorials to St. Paul Lutheran Church of Lockport appreciated.

Obituaries often list the names of the deceased's relatives, along with dates of death, age, and burial information.

G

Name:	Misao Abe
Birth Date:	abt 1892
Birth Place:	Japan
Age:	23
Death Date:	5 Dec 1915
Funeral Home:	Martin and Brown Funeral Directors

While few in number, funeral home records can be useful.

RESEARCH GOAL: *Determine an ancestor's birth date by using non-vital records.*

STEP ❶ Use the age field in federal censuses.

Beginning in 1850, the federal census gave the age for everyone in the household (**A**), allowing you to count backwards to establish a potential birth year. For example, if the 1860 census gave an age of forty-five, you know by simple subtraction that the year of birth was around 1815.

Enumerators used fractions (**B**) to record ages for people born within the census year: 1/12 (one month old), 2/12 (two months old), etc. Going back from the date the census was taken, you can get very close to the exact month the person was born.

STEP ❷ Search in military records.

The WWI draft registration cards and documents from the WWII "Old Man's Draft" include actual birth dates, as do other kinds of military records. See chapter 4 for more.

A

①

B

②

REGISTRATION CARD—(Men born on or after April 28, 1877 and on or before February 16, 1897)			
SERIAL NUMBER U 3150	1. NAME (Print) Arthur (First) R (Initial only) (Middle) hiebig (Last)		ORDER NUMBER
2 PLACE OF RESIDENCE (Print) 1930 Earle Ave (Number and street) Rosemead (Town, township, village, or city) h. A (County) Calif. (State)			
[THE PLACE OF RESIDENCE GIVEN ON THE LINE ABOVE WILL DETERMINE LOCAL BOARD JURISDICTION; LINE 2 OF REGISTRATION CERTIFICATE WILL BE IDENTICAL]			
3. MAILING ADDRESS Same [Mailing address if other than place indicated on line 2. If same insert word same]		in W. S. A. 54 yr naturalized	
4. TELEPHONE AT 2-8688	5. AGE IN YEARS 64 DATE OF BIRTH Sept 22 1877	6. PLACE OF BIRTH thru father Saxeony (Town or county) Germany	

③

STATE OF MISSOURI, SS.
COUNTY OF JACKSON.

This License authorizes any Judge, Justice of the Peace, licensed or ordained Preacher of the Gospel, who is a citizen of the United States, or other person authorized under the laws of this State to solemnize marriage between Hershel B. Hendrickson *of the County of* Jackson *and State of* Mo *who is* over *the age of twenty-one years and* Bessie F. Faulkenberry *of the County of* Jackson *and State of* mo *who is* over *the age of eighteen years*

Witness my hand as Recorder, with the seal of office hereto affixed, at my office in Independence, Missouri, this 12 *day of* April 1913

R H Bowler RECORDER
By Edgar G Hinde DEPUTY RECORDER

STEP ③ Look for marriage certificates.

These usually include the ages of the bride and groom. If not, they may indicate if the person was over a certain age (e.g., over the age of twenty-one).

STEP ④ Consult tombstones,

Headstones often include a date of birth or (at least) the year of birth. You may also find a tombstone inscription such as: aged 57 years, 4 months, 18 days. In order to calculate the birth date from this information, you could do the math. However, there are several online sites that will automatically calculate the date of birth for you. You can find several at Cyndi's List <**www.cyndislist.com/calendars/birthdate-calendars-and-calculators**>.

④

SNOW
WILLIAM F. SNOW
BORN JAN. 29, 1825
DIED NOV. 30, 1903
LOUISA J. WIFE OF
Wᴹ F. SNOW
BORN MAR. 18, 1828
DIED MAR. 21, 1898.
BLESSED ARE THE DEAD THAT DIE IN THE LORD

EXERCISE ② Finding and Analyzing Marriage Records

RESEARCH GOAL: *Find a marriage record for Stephen I. Snow and Mary Jane Shore.*

STEP ❶ Enter your search terms.

Click Search on the main Ancestry.com menu, then select Birth, Marriage & Death. Add as much information as possible to the search form, such as names, places, and approximate year of birth (**A**). My search resulted in more than forty-eight thousand hits. Interestingly, the top choices bore no resemblance to my query! However, on the results list (**B**), my ancestor was under the "These records are less likely to match your search but may be helpful. Edit your search or learn more." (Note the name Shore is misspelled as *Share*—a cautionary tale!)

A   ❶

First & Middle Name(s)	Last Name
Stephen	Snow
☐ Exact…	☐ Exact…

	Day	Month	Year	Location
Birth	▼	▼	1830	north carolina
			☐ Exact +/-…	☐ Exact
Lived In	——	——	——	City, County, State, Countr
Marriage	▼	▼		Missouri, USA
				☐ Exact to…
Any Event	——	▼		City, County, State, Countr

Add family member: Father   Mother   Spouse   Child

	First & Middle Name(s)	Last Name	
Father			✕
Mother	Mary	shore	✕
	▣ Exact	▣ Exact	

B

> 📄 **Missouri, Marriage Records, 1805-2002**
> MARRIAGE & DIVORCE
>
> View Image

NAME: **Stephen J Snow**
SPOUSE: Mary J Share
MARRIAGE: 3 Jan 1856 - Lafayette, Missouri, USA
CIVIL: Lafayette, Missouri, USA

STEP ② View your images.

Click on the View Image link. The image was extremely difficult to read (**A**). But I could read enough to get the names and dates of the record.

But what if you find an image so light you can barely read it? Ancestry.com gives you the option to invert the image (make black look like white and vice versa). You'll find this option by clicking the tool icon on the right side of the page (**B**).

STEP ③ Search more broadly.

Look to other records to confirm what you've found (or if you can't find the marriage record). Go to a federal census taken after you *think* the marriage took place. In this case, I went to the 1860 census.

As you can see, Stephen and Mary had a three-year-old and a one-year-old. Using subtraction, I can assume that the marriage took place in either 1856 or 1857. This is just a guess, but a logical one.

A   **②**   **B**

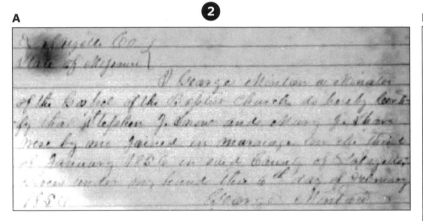

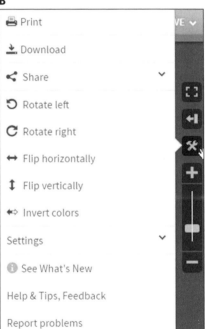

③

1715	1778	Stephen I. Snow		3 9	m
		Mary	"	23	f
		Elleonora	"	3	f
		Dora	"	1	f

EXERCISE ③ Finding a Gravesite

RESEARCH GOAL: *Find a gravesite for Rachel Knox (1787–1871).*

STEP ❶ Find your collection.

Go to the Card Catalog and filter for Birth, Marriage & Death. Then type *mortality* in the Keyword(s) box. Of the six resultant collections, I selected "Missouri, Federal Census Mortality Schedules Index, 1850 and 1860."

STEP ❷ Enter your search terms.

Hopefully you'll know the name, date of birth, and approximate date of death. More important (for me) is knowing the place of death. That way, if I can't find an online record of a gravesite, I can contact cemeteries in the area that might have the information I need.

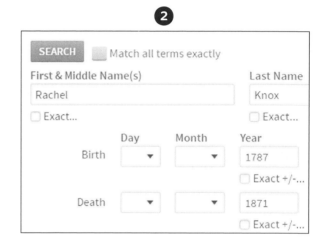

STEP ❸ Review your results.

In this instance, the first two hits were for my ancestor (**A**). The first result gave me an overview of her cemetery record. The second search result (**B**) was from the Find A Grave <www.findagrave.com>. There, I found a photo of the cemetery, but not of Rachel's grave. However, I did find more information as Rachel's information had a link to the burial of her husband, Joseph. His bio read, "Iowa Pioneer considered the 'Father of Sigourney,' a leading merchant and active in Keokuk politics. Married Rachel Brooks (d.11 Sep 1871) April 9, 1807. Father of fifteen children."

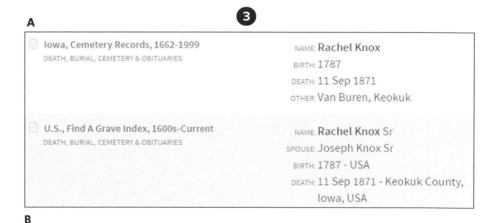

A

Iowa, Cemetery Records, 1662-1999
DEATH, BURIAL, CEMETERY & OBITUARIES

NAME: **Rachel Knox**
BIRTH: 1787
DEATH: 11 Sep 1871
OTHER: Van Buren, Keokuk

U.S., Find A Grave Index, 1600s-Current
DEATH, BURIAL, CEMETERY & OBITUARIES

NAME: **Rachel Knox** Sr
SPOUSE: Joseph Knox Sr
BIRTH: 1787 - USA
DEATH: 11 Sep 1871 - Keokuk County, Iowa, USA

B

Name:	Rachel Knox
Birth Date:	1787
Death Date:	11 Sep 1871
Age:	84
Burial Location:	Van Buren, Keokuk
Cemetery:	Johnson
General Burial Info:	(Mrs. J.)
Source:	Gravestone Records of Keokuk County, Iowa
Page Number:	116

STEP ④ Find other resources.

Although I didn't end up with a photo of Rachel's tombstone on Ancestry.com, I did learn a lot about her husband and the number of children they had. Next, I used the GPS coordinates of the cemetery and did a flyover using Google Earth **<www.google.com/earth>**. What I saw was a very small country cemetery—one I hope to visit.

Find A Grave allows you to submit a photo request. I clicked on the requests and saw that someone had already requested photos of Rachel and Joseph's tombstone. The request couldn't be fulfilled; according to the volunteer (who had posted on the site): "I searched the entire cemetery and could not find the grave. There are a large number of stones that can't be read and I think that there are some missing stones." Although that tombstone photo will never be taken, at least I know where the family was buried.

(Odd fact: Did you know there's a word for people who are interested in cemeteries and tombstones? They're called taphophiles!)

RESEARCH GOAL: *Find death records for Bessie Hendrickson.*

STEP ❶ Find your collection.

Follow Step 1 from Exercise #3 and fill in the form. This is one of those cases in which I would add, not only name, date, and place, but also the name of the spouse (if any). That's because the spouse's name is almost always on the death certificate.

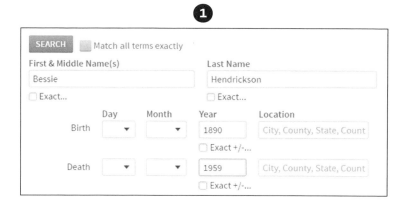

STEP ❷ Decide which results best meet the research goals.

The top two results are from Find A Grave; I know where Bessie is buried, so this didn't meet my needs. But about a dozen results lower was one from "Missouri Death Records" that I knew was for her, as it matched her exact name and death date. The strange thing, though, is that she died in *Kansas*, not Missouri.

When I clicked on the link it took me off-site to the Missouri Digital Heritage site <www.sos.mo.gov/mdh>. When I clicked on the More Information button it took me to another page letting me know that this Missouri resident had died out of state. I also learned that I had to contact the state of Kansas for more information.

STEP ❸ Continue searching as needed.

As none of the other results were relevant, I next went to the Card Catalog and used filters to search for a Kansas-specific death collection. Another failure. There were several Kansas collections, but they were either from the wrong county, wrong time frame, or of people who were buried in Kansas (Bessie was not). Some searches end like this one.

But not all was lost. Among the many search results was a link to Bessie's marriage records, which included an image of the actual record. As for her death records: My next step will be to write to a Kansas archive.

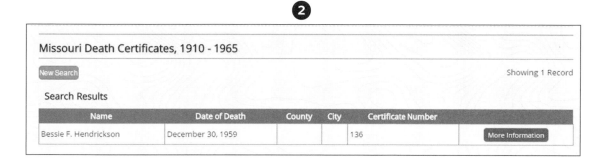

EXERCISE ⑤ Verifying Information from a Death Record with Other Sources

RESEARCH GOAL: *Confirm death date and other important information using other sources.*

As mentioned earlier in this chapter, death records aren't foolproof. (The Research and Records Checklists in appendix B describe resources to consult for vital information.) If you suspect death record information in particular is inaccurate, you can try to verify it by going to the following types of records:

❶ CENSUS

- Date of birth (by subtracting the age from the year of the census; see Exercise #1)
- State or country of birth of the person
- State or country of birth of the parents

PERSON.		FATHER.		MOTHER
Place of birth.	Mother tongue.	Place of birth.	Mother tongue.	Place of birth.
19	20	21	22	23
New York		Pennsylvania		New York
Pennsylvania		Pennsylvania		Pennsylvania
Pennsylvania		England	English	England
Pennsylvania		New York		Pennsylvania

❷ MARRIAGE RECORDS

- Place of marriage (which might also be place of birth)
- Age
- Name of spouse
- Name of parents

No. 9044

Marriage License.

Office of Recorder of Deeds, Jackson County, Missouri, at Independence.

STATE OF MISSOURI, ￫ ss. COUNTY OF JACKSON. ￫ This License authorizes any Judge, Justice of the Peace, Licensed or Ordained Preacher of the Gospel, who is a citizen of the United States, or other person authorized under the laws of this State, to solemnize marriage between *Herschel B. Hendrickson* of the County of *Jackson* and State of *Missouri* who is *over* the age of twenty-one years and *Bessie F. Fauldenberry* of the County of *Jackson* and State of *Missouri* who is *over* the age of eighteen years.

WITNESS my hand as Recorder, with the seal of office hereto affixed, at my office in Independence, Missouri, this *12th* day of *April* 1913. *P.H. Bowler* Recorder.

STATE OF MISSOURI, ￫ ss. COUNTY OF JACKSON. ￫ By *J.A. Flanagan* Deputy Recorder.

This is to certify that the undersigned, *Minister of Gospel* did, in said County and State, on the *9th* day of *April* A. D. 1913, unite in marriage the above named persons. *Leslie M. Lucas Lees Summit Mo*

Filed for Record and duly Recorded in my office this *10th* day of *May* A. D. 1913. *P.H. Bowler* Recorder.

By *J.A. Flanagan* Deputy Recorder.

❸ MILITARY RECORDS

- Age
- Date of birth
- Place of birth

AGE 1st July, 1863.	WHITE OR COLORED.	DESCRIPTION. PROFESSION. OCCUPATION, OR TRADE.	PLACE OF BIRTH. (Naming the State, Territory, or Country.)
38	White	Farmer	Can'd
39	"	"	Ky
36	"	Merchant	Germany

❹ BIRTH RECORDS

- Age
- Place of birth
- Name of parents
- Age of parents

Name:	David Lyle Hendrickson
Birth Date:	14 Apr 1910
Birth Place:	Hancock, Iowa, United States
Father:	Magnes Lars Hendrickson
Mother:	Delia Richardson
FHL Film Number:	1477109

❺ SOCIAL SECURITY DEATH INDEX, APPLICATIONS & CLAIMS (SSDI)

- Age
- Place of birth
- Date of birth
- Name of parents
- Maiden name of mother

Name:	Herschel Byron Hendrickson
Gender:	Male
Race:	White
Birth Date:	18 Aug 1888
Birth Place:	Jackson Coun, Missouri
Father:	James Hendrickson
Mother:	Ella Snow
Type of Claim:	Original SSN.
Notes:	30 Dec 1983: Name listed as HERSCHEL BYRON HENDRICKSON

➤ Narrow your search for marriage records by searching census records for the age and birth-place of the first child.

➤ Use city directories to narrow death dates. Once the husband has died, the wife is usually still listed in them as "widow" or "wid."

➤ Search probate records for birth dates, death dates, and ages and names of children.

➤ Consider the timing of children's births. If you find a wide gap in the ages of the children, this might be the result of the death of the first wife and the marriage to a second. In addition, children were typically born about two years apart. Use this information to estimate birth dates.

➤ Look for other people with the same surname who are married in the same locale when search-ing for your ancestors' marriage records. You might find that one of them is a sibling of your direct ancestor, which could provide valuable information for your current research question.

BIRTH RECORD ABSTRACT FORM

Use this form to transcribe information from birth records and indexes you find on Ancestry.com. Fill in whatever information you discover, as well as where the information comes from.

Ancestor information

Name:_____ Date of birth: _____

Gender: M   F   Twin, triplet, or other?: _____   Legitimate?:   Y   N

Place of birth

Country:_____ State: _____ County _____

City: _____ Parish: _____

Parent information

Mother's name: _____

Age/date of birth:_____ Race: _____

Birthplace: _____ Occupation: _____

Father's name: _____

Age/date of birth _____ Race: _____

Birthplace: _____ Occupation: _____

Place of residence: _____ Number of living children: _____

Source information

Collection name: _____ Date filed: _____

Collection source (index, courthouse, etc.): _____ Date accessed: _____

BIRTH INFORMATION SOURCE TRACKER

Use this form to track information you find about your ancestors' birth dates, and compare facts provided by multiple sources. See the Records Checklists in appendix B for sources to consult when researching birth information.

Ancestor name	Name of collection/ home source	Date of birth (or estimate)	Location of birth	Saved to family tree?	Notes

MARRIAGE RECORD ABSTRACT FORM

Use this form to transcribe information from marriage indexes you find on Ancestry.com.

Bride information

Name:_____

Date of birth:_____ Age of marriage: _____ Birthplace: _____

Occupation: _____ Residence: _____ Race: _____

Father's name: _____ Mother's name:_____

Previous spouse(s): _____

Children (if any) and their ages:_____

Groom information

Name:_____

Date of birth:_____ Age of marriage: _____ Birthplace: _____

Occupation: _____ Residence: _____ Race: _____

Father's name: _____ Mother's name:_____

Previous spouse(s): _____

Children (if any) and their ages:_____

Place of marriage

Country: _____ State:_____ County: _____

City: _____ Parish/courthouse: _____

Source information

Collection name: _____ Date filed: _____

Collection source (index, courthouse, etc.): _____ Date accessed: _____

MARRIAGE INFORMATION SOURCE TRACKER

Use this form to track information you find about your ancestors' marriages, and compare facts provided by multiple sources. See the Records Checklists in appendix B for sources to consult when researching marriage information.

Names of the bride and groom	Name of collection/ home source	Date of marriage (or estimate)	Location of marriage	Saved to family tree?	Notes

DEATH RECORD ABSTRACT FORM

Use this form to transcribe information from death records such as death certificates and obituaries.

Ancestor information

Name: _____ Date of death:_____

Gender: M F   Cause of death: _____ Date of burial: _____

Marital status:_____ Name of spouse(s): _____

Date of birth: _____ Age of death: _____ Birthplace: _____

Occupation:_____ Race: _____

Place of death

Country:_____ State: _____ County:_____

City: _____Parish: _____   _____

Parent information

Mother's name: _____

Age/date of birth: _____ Race: _____

Birthplace: _____Occupation: _____

Place of residence: _____Number of children living: _____

Father's name: _____

Age/date of birth: _____ Race: _____

Birthplace: _____Occupation: _____

Place of residence: _____Number of children living: _____

Source information

Collection name: _____ Date filed: _____

Collection source (index, courthouse, etc.): _____ Date accessed: _____

DEATH INFORMATION SOURCE TRACKER

Use this form to track information you find about ancestors' deaths, and compare facts provided by multiple sources. See the Records Checklists in appendix B for sources to consult when researching death information.

Ancestor name	Name of collection/ home source	Date of death (or estimate)	Location of death	Saved to family tree?	Notes

MILITARY RECORDS

If your ancestor was born in the United States from 1720 to the present, he (or she, in more recent conflicts) may have served in the military, leaving behind a trove of records. In the many years I've worked on my family tree, I've found military records to be invaluable. They can place an ancestor in a specific place at a specific time—much like state and federal censuses. But more than that, once you've located your ancestor in a military regiment or company within the regiment, you can then go to other sources to flesh out the details of his service. I'll give you an example later in this chapter.

There are nine subcategories of military records within Ancestry.com:

1. Draft, Enlistment, and Service
2. Casualties
3. Soldier, Veteran & Prisoner Rolls & Lists
4. Pension Records
5. Histories
6. Awards & Decorations of Honor
7. News
8. Disciplinary Actions
9. Photos

Although Ancestry.com's military-related collections number over one thousand, what can you realistically expect to find? Some of Ancestry.com's most popular military resources for each conflict are:

- **Revolutionary War:** Bounty land warrants, service records, pensions, rolls, Sons of the American Revolution (SAR) membership applications, Daughters of the American Revolutionary (DAR) lineage books

- **War of 1812:** Muster rolls, pension application index, service records

- **Mexican-American War:** Military service records of American volunteer soldiers

- **Civil War:** Pension index, draft registrations, Civil War regiments, Civil War photos, Regular Army enlistments, state-specific collections

- **Spanish-American War:** Volunteer soldier index, index to service records

- **World War I:** Draft registration cards, soldier naturalizations, state-specific collections

- **World War II:** "Old Man's Draft," Army enlistment records, Navy and Marine muster rolls, draft cards (partial)

Note that the Korean War, Vietnam War, and more recent conflicts have few records beyond gravesite collections.

Military is the one category of Ancestry.com records that goes hand-in-hand with sister site Fold3 <www.fold3.com>. If military research is of great importance to you, consider a free trial subscription to Fold3, or get half off your Fold3 subscription as an Ancestry.com subscriber. Images found at Fold3 can be saved to your Ancestry.com family tree.

GETTING STARTED

As with any search you perform on Ancestry.com, you'll need to identify a specific set of records and a time period in which to conduct your search for military records. In this section, I'll discuss three questions to ask yourself so you'll find the right collection(s) of military records to search.

Question 1: Which War?

Before you begin searching for military records, use this chart to learn which war your ancestor might have served in. Note that these birth years are approximate, and dates of conflict are based on dates of US involvement.

Name of conflict	Dates	Birth year
Revolutionary War	1775-1783	1720-1765
War of 1812	1812-1815	1757-1798
Mexican-American War	1846-1848	1791-1831
Civil War	1861-1865	1806-1848
Spanish-American War	1898	1843-1881
World War I	1917-1918	1862-1901
World War II	1941-1945	1886-1928
Korean War	1950-1953	1895-1936
Vietnam War	1965-1973	1904-1958

Question 2: Which Subcategories?

Although there are nine subcategories of military records, only six kinds of records will comprise your primary search:

1. Draft
2. Enlistment
3. Service
4. Casualties
5. Soldier, Veteran & Prisoner Rolls & Lists
6. Pensions

Note that, even though Draft, Enlistment, and Service are lumped together as a single Ancestry.com subcategory, each has unique information.

DRAFT

Draft records include those who served as well as those who never served, and these records often include large portions of the male population. More than twenty-four million men registered for the draft between 1917 and 1918, close to 25 percent of the total US population at the time.

Draft registration cards can include an address, physical description, occupation, and age. Image **A** shows the first page of a WWI 1917 draft registration form. The second page (not shown) gives a physical description of the registrant as well as the date and county where the registration was done. See the Military Draft Records Worksheet at the end of this chapter to record information from this type of resource.

Depending on the time period and conflict, your ancestor may appear in draft records even if he wasn't of fighting age at the time. Six separate drafts were held during World War II: five for men born between 1897 and 1927, and a sixth, known as the "Old Man's Draft," that was taken in 1942 and included men aged forty-five to sixty-four (born between April 27, 1877, and February 16, 1890). This draft registration was not for drafting men into military service, but rather to determine manpower capability for wartime production needs. Although Ancestry.com has a searchable collection of the Old Man's Draft, records from Alabama, Florida, Georgia, Kentucky, Mississippi, North Carolina, South Carolina, and Tennessee have been destroyed.

Note: Your ancestor may appear in both the WWI and WWII draft registrations if he was born between 1877 and 1900.

A

Even if your ancestor didn't serve in the military, his draft registration can provide information about his life.

Searching for Bounty Land Warrants—and What They Mean

If your ancestor was in military service pre-1858, be sure to search the collection of bounty land warrants <search.ancestry.com/search/db.aspx?dbid=1165>. Bounty land warrants—gifts of free land—were used as incentives or compensations to soldiers. The Warrants date from colonial days (1789) up to 1858.

You'll find the bounty land warrant collection either via the link above or by using the Card Catalog. In addition, Fold3 provides a free index of Bounty Land Warrant applications for the War of 1812, the Mexican-American War, and early Indian Wars.

If you find a Bounty Land Warrant you'll be able to tell your ancestor's military rank:

- 100 acres: private or noncommissioned officer
- 150 acres: ensign
- 200 acres: lieutenant
- 300 acres: captain
- 400 acres: major
- 450 acres: lieutenant colonel
- 500 acres: colonel
- 850 acres: brigadier general
- 1100 acres: major general

The image at right is of a bounty land warrant for Revolutionary War service. You'll note the soldier, as a private, received one hundred acres and that his land was in "any of the Districts appropriate for satisfying the Bounties of Land." The federal government and states reserved land in the public domain for this purpose. A bit of historical knowledge reveals that this Virginia veteran received land in Ohio because, at the time, all Virginia bounty land was in the present-day states of Kentucky and Ohio.

Bounty land warrants, like the one above, provide information about your military ancestor and his service.

ENLISTMENT

Enlistment records include information on men who actively enlisted in military service. During the Civil War, you'll find ancestors volunteering for service in state-raised regiments, such as the 27th Indiana. WWII enlistment records include vital statistics as well as branch of service, term of enlistment, occupation, rank, and education.

SERVICE

Information from these records varies, but can include (in Civil War records) whether a soldier was present or absent, the amount of bounty paid, a place of birth, and information about any wounds he incurred. War of 1812 service records will give information on company, rank, and the National Archives and Records Administration (NARA) microfilm and roll box numbers. Use the company name (if given) to flesh out further research (e.g., *Capt. Herrod's Co., Mtd. Riflemen (1812), Ohio Militia*).

CASUALTIES

Ancestry.com casualty records can reveal information about soldiers killed in action as well as the location of US veteran gravesites. The killed-in-action collections are not restricted to US soldiers; they also include UK and Irish casualties from World War I as well as German losses in the Franco-Prussian War.

During your search, you may find a discrepancy between the date of death and the date of interment (image **B**). In this instance, the reason for the four-year span is that the person was originally interred in Europe and later re-interred in the United States.

In a case such as this, following Ancestry.com suggestions (image **C**) can prove invaluable.

B

Name:	Raymond E Herr
Birth Date:	24 Feb 1920
Death Date:	22 Sep 1944
Interment Date:	14 Dec 1948
Cemetery:	Ft. Leavenworth National Cemetery
Cemetery Address:	Fort Leavenworth, KS 66027
Buried At:	Section I Site 229-K

SAVE ⌄   Cancel

Discrepancies in dates stated in records may seem like mistakes, but they can actually provide interesting insights into an ancestor's life.

C

Suggested Records ❓

📄 U.S. Veterans Gravesites, ca.1775-2006
Raymond E Herr

📄 1930 United States Federal Census
Raymond E Herr

📄 U.S. National Cemetery Interment Control Forms, 1928-1962
Raymond E Herr

📄 Pennsylvania, Veteran Compensation Application Files, WWII, 1950-1966
Raymond Harvey Herr

Ancestry.com provides suggested records with each of your military searches. These can open up new avenues of research.

The "U.S. National Cemetery Interment Control Forms" collection shows the date and authorization of re-interment.

SOLDIER, VETERAN & PRISONER ROLLS & LISTS

This group contains a wide variety of military records from veterans' homes, directories, muster rolls, and enlistment records. This is exactly the type of category to search when you've completed the most "logical" military searches. In some cases, the information here might wrap up loose ends or open new lines of inquiry.

Collections include applications for military headstones and Sons of the American Revolution membership applications. If your ancestor was stationed in the United States, don't miss "U.S., Select Military Registers, 1862–1985."

PENSION

Ancestry.com has a variety of records; some include pension applications, and others are simply an index of applicants. Image **D** gives you an example of the information included on a pension index card. The index can show (as in this example) that the veteran himself applied for a pension in 1907 as an invalid, and that his widow applied for a widow's pension in 1917. The index card shows the Civil War regiment in which he served and the state he was living in when he filed for a pension. See the Military Pension Records Worksheet at the end of this chapter to record information from this type of resource.

Question 3: Which Other Subcategories?

Don't disregard these last five subcategories just because they don't have official service records. Here you can find details not related to actual service or pension files. But these types of records add a more personal touch, such as details of battles in which your ancestor fought or photos of a typical Civil War regiment.

Military Service Clues in Census Records

In addition to the 1890 veterans' schedule, you can find military clues hidden in the 1910 and 1930 federal census records.

1910 census: Look for column 30. This will indicate whether a person was a "survivor of the Union or Confederal Army or Navy." The shorthand answers were: *UA* (Union Army), *UN* (Union Navy), *CA* (Confederate Army), and *CN* (Confederate Navy). Don't be confused by columns 30–32, which can be overwritten with numbers. Per the Census Bureau, these numbers have no bearing on military service information.

1930 census: The 1930 census had two military-related columns. One (column 30) asked if the person was a veteran of a war or conflict, and the other (column 31) asked for the name of the war or expedition. Civil War veterans were noted with the abbreviation *CW*. Other possible abbreviations were *Sp* (Spanish-American War), *Phil* (Philippine Insurrection), *Box* (Boxer Rebellion), *Mex* (Mexican Expedition), and *WW* (World War I).

D

NAME OF SOLDIER:		Dimmitt, Calvin M.		(3-H-3)
NAME OF DEPENDENT:	Widow,	Dimmitt, Nancy L.		
	Minor,			
SERVICE:		H 7 Tenn. Mt'd Inf.		

DATE OF FILING.	CLASS.	APPLICATION NO.	CERTIFICATE NO.	STATE FROM WHICH FILED.
190? Feb. 28	Invalid,	1 3 5 8 9 8 4	1 1 3 7 1 6 6	Mo.
1917 Feb. 17	Widow,	1 0 9 3. 8 1 6	8 2 6 5 7 8	Mo.

Pension records can indicate who and when your military ancestors and their relatives applied for a pension.

After searching through the primary records, use these remaining categories for secondary searches:

1. **Histories:** Learn the details of military engagements and campaigns.

2. **Awards & Decorations of Honor:** Here you'll find information about awards presented to members of the military to commemorate service.

3. **News:** As the name implies, this includes historical news, including information on specific regiments.

4. **Disciplinary Actions:** Don't miss this one, particularly if your ancestor went to West Point or Annapolis or was a Loyalist during the American Revolution.

5. **Photos:** You may not find your ancestor, but it's possible you'll find an image of his regiment, a battle in which he fought, or a similar unit (e.g., Civil War artillery unit).

Using Records from the Daughters of the American Revolution

I went to the Daughters of the American Revolution database <services.dar.org/public/dar_research/search/?Tab_ID=1> to see if any of my ancestors had ever applied for membership using my ancestor Benjamin's military service. They had, and I could see some information (name, rank, state, estimates of birth and death dates, and brief descriptions of service) for free.

If I wanted to download the actual member application used to prove this patriot line, I could pay ten dollars. But for now, I have plenty of information to keep my research busy. Going to Google <www.google.com>, I looked up Captains Henry Heath and Uriah Springer as well as Colonel John Gibson and the 7th Virginia Continent Line. As you can imagine, I found a treasure trove of service information including a history of the regiment at FamilySearch.org <www.familysearch.org> and

Wikipedia <www.wikipedia.org>. This regiment took part in the Battle of Brandywine, the Battle of Germantown, the Battle of Monmouth, and the Siege of Charleston. Just researching those four events would fill up a whole notebook.

But is there more to find? Using the DAR information, I saw that Benjamin died in 1809 in Highland County, Ohio. I went back to Google and searched for *history of highland county ohio*. A free book came up in search results, and it had an embarrassment of riches about Benjamin and his family.

My favorite was the story about the family building a canoe and going down the Ohio, only to sink not far down the river and lose most of their belongings. However, they made their way up the Scioto River to "near Chillicothe." Using Google Maps <www.google.com/maps>, I could trace their journey. How cool is that?

RESEARCH GOAL: *Discover Civil War pension records for Francis Gibson, who lived in Pennsylvania and Indiana.*

STEP ❶ Search for a collection.

Go to the Card Catalog. Because Ancestry.com has pension records for more than one conflict, I narrowed down the parameters by filtering for Military > USA > 1860s.

STEP ❷ Enter your search terms.

I entered *pension* into the Keyword(s) box.

①

Title

Keyword(s)

SEARCH   or   Clear All

Filter Titles

❌ Military

❌ USA

❌ 1860s

②

Title	Results 1-9 of 9		Sort By	Popularity

Title
pension

Keyword(s)

SEARCH   or   Clear All

Filter Titles
❌ Military
❌ USA
❌ 1860s

Search entire "Military" Category

Title	Collection	Records	A
📄 U.S., Civil War Pension Index: General Index to Pension Files, 1861-1934	Military	2,313,984	
📄 U.S., Revolutionary War Pension and Bounty-Land Warrant Application Files, 1800-1900	Military	83,050	
📄 Alabama, Confederate Pension and Service Records, 1862-1947	Military	1,950,072	
📄 U.S., Civil War and Later Wars Index to Remarried Widow Pension Applications, 1860-1934	Military	51,536	

STEP ❸ Begin searching.

I selected "U.S., Civil War Pension Index." Because I didn't have any relevant dates to add to the search box, I just typed in Francis' first name, last name, wife's first name, and state. This returned more than two thousand results—too many to search through. What to do next?

If you have any additional information, this is the time to add it to the search box in order to filter down results. I added the middle initial *M*, which narrowed down to 224 results. That's probably still too many to go through, but thanks to Ancestry.com's built-in mechanism for analysis, the system alerts me to the fact that the first six results were most likely the ones I was searching.

③

Results 1–10 of 224

View Record	Name	Widow	State Filed	View Image
View Record	Francis Gibson	Fannie M Gibson	Indiana	🗐
View Record	Alonzo M Gibson	Mary J Gibson	Indiana	🗐
View Record	James M Gibson		Indiana	🗐
View Record	Lawrence M Gibson	Nellie Gibson	Indiana	🗐
View Record	Thomas M Gibson		Indiana	🗐
View Record	Albert F Gibson	Hattie M Gibson	Indiana	🗐

These records are less likely to match your search but may be helpful. Edit your search or learn more.

View Record	Francis M Gibson	Julia A Gibson	Kentucky	🗐
View Record	Francis M Gibson	Lucy C Gibson	Ohio and California	🗐
View Record	James R Gibson	Anna M Gibson	Indiana and Illinois	🗐
View Record	John Gibson	Ruth M Gibson	Indiana	🗐

STEP ❹ Review your results and conduct more research.

I clicked on the first result and felt fairly confident that this is the person I'm searching for. The record shows his wife, Fannie, filed for a widow's pension from the state of Indiana. It also shows Francis' service was in a Pennsylvania regiment.

Although Ancestry.com's Civil War pension records only include index cards, I now had more information to feed further research. What did it tell me?

• Gibson was still alive in 1891 when he filed for "invalid" status.

• Gibson's widow was alive in 1919.

• Gibson served in three Civil War regiments.

• Both his original and his widow's pensions were filed in the state of Indiana.

• His wife's middle initial was *M*.

If Francis Gibson were your ancestor, what would you do next? Research the history of the three regiments in which he served: the 71th PA Infantry, the 69th PA Infantry, and the 19th PA Infantry. You can do this in the "American Civil War Regiments, 1861–1865" collection, which includes information on all of the battles fought by each regiment.

Once you have this knowledge, your possible next steps include:

• Search the 1910 federal censuses (Indiana and Pennsylvania) to see if you can find Francis and Fannie.

• Search the 1890 veterans schedule. Francis himself applied for a pension in 1891, so hopefully he can be found on the 1890 veterans schedule.

• Search the Military > Photos collections for images of Civil War regiments as well as battles in which I knew Gibson's regiments had fought. (I found several.)

• Search the Military > News category for information on one of the major battles in which the 69th PA took part: Fredericksburg. Within the collection of Abraham Lincoln papers were telegrams sent during the battle itself, relaying troop movements (e.g., "Franklin Corps trying to flank the enemy").

Who knew that a tiny index card could lead to such research breakthroughs?

❹

EXERCISE ② Finding an Ancestor's WWI Draft Registration

RESEARCH GOAL: *Find Herschel Hendrickson in the WWI draft registration.*

STEP ❶ Find your collection and enter search terms.

Type *World War I Draft Registration* into the search Title box (**A**). Choose your collection. I clicked on the collection and entered the first and last names, date, and state of birth of my ancestor, Herschel Hendrickson (**B**).

STEP ❷ View your results.

Although the search resulted in more than eighteen hundred names, the one I was searching for came up first. Click on the name to bring up a summary of his record. Note that the record can be saved to your Ancestry.com family tree by clicking the green Save button.

STEP ❸ Study the scanned record.

Click on the green View button to see the actual draft registration card. As you can see, the card gives an address, occupation, and place of employment. It also notes that he was supporting a wife and child. And I could see his actual signature—what a bonus. It was far neater than my own! The second part of the image (not shown) gives a physical description: stout build, medium height, blue eyes, and brown hair. As he died when I was less than a year old, all I had ever seen were old black-and-white photos, so it was a nice surprise to learn that we share our blue eyes.

A

B

EXERCISE ③ Searching for an Ancestor on the Main Military Form

RESEARCH GOAL: *Find information on John Strange using military records.*

STEP ❶ Conduct your search.

Choose Military from the main navigation menu and type in search information. I filled in John's name and where I knew he lived. I didn't know his birth date, but I was certain he served in the Civil War.

STEP ❷ Evaluate your results.

All three first results were excellent (**A**), but I knew that the first one was the ancestor I was searching for. They were fascinating; not only did I learn which regiment John served with, but I could also see his rank and his disability (**B**).

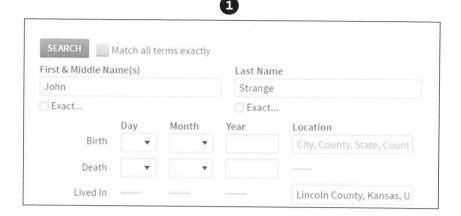

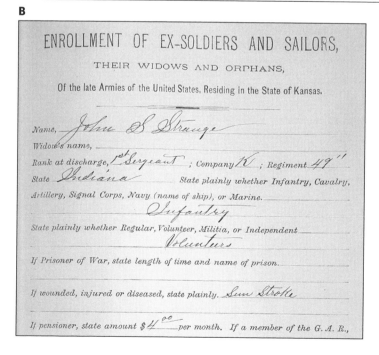

STEP ❸ Conduct further research using other resources.

Further resources you can use to learn more about this ancestor include the 1890 veterans schedule (though John Strange's home state, Kansas, is not included here) or movements of individual regiments. For example, I could go to Military > Histories and find "American Civil War Regiments, 1861–1866," then search for the 49th Indiana Infantry. Ancestry.com provides a summary of the regiment. Use the summary and a map to trace the 49th Indiana's Civil War movements, which will take you from Jeffersonville, Indiana, in 1861 to Louisville, Kentucky, in 1865. The summary also includes various regimental duties, from battles to canal digging. Once you begin reading the 49th's journey (and see how much manual labor the 49th did in the sun), you'll understand Strange's diagnosis of sun stroke.

No Image Text-only collection	
🖊 Add alternate information	
⚠ Report issue	

Regiment:	49th Infantry Regiment Indiana
Date of Organization:	21 Nov 1861
Muster Date:	13 Sep 1865
Regiment State:	Indiana
Regiment Type:	Infantry
Regiment Number:	49th
Officers Killed or Mortally Wounded:	1
Officers Died of Disease or Accident:	3
Enlisted Killed or Mortally Wounded:	40
Enlisted Died of Disease or Accident:	192
Battles:	Fought on 28 Dec 1862 at Chickasaw Bayou, MS. Fought on 29 Dec 1862 at Chickasaw Bayou, MS. Fought on 1 May 1863 at Port Gibson, MS. Fought on 16 May 1863 at Champion's Hill, MS. Fought on 16 May 1863 at Baker's Creek, MS. Fought on 19 May 1863 at Vicksburg, MS.

➤ Consider history and choose your search terms accordingly. For example, the "United States" didn't exist during the Revolutionary War. Rather, a Revolutionary War soldier either belonged to a state militia or the volunteer Continental Army (which evolved into the US Army). As a result, if you're using the Card Catalog to narrow down searchable collections, remember to include the state in which he lived in your search. Likewise, during the Civil War, soldiers typically served in state regiments as volunteers or in the Regular Army.

➤ Add *Navy*, *Naval*, *Army*, *Air Force*, or *Marine* to the Card Catalog Title field if searching for a collection for a particular branch of the service.

➤ Use the Card Catalog filters to narrow down to Military Records and decade of the conflict if you're searching for collections for a specific war or conflict.

➤ Search the 1890 veterans schedule, which is available for the states alphabetically between Kentucky (partial) through Wyoming. The collection includes name, rank, regiment, company, dates of enlistment and discharge, and length of service. When using the 1890 veterans schedule, scroll down to the bottom of the page to find notes about any disability. The line number for the disability corresponds to the same line number on which your ancestor is listed. For example, James Knox was listed on line 19 of the census page. Scrolling down to the bottom of the page, line 19 of the bottom section shows me that he received a wound in the knee.

➤ Check Service records if your Civil War soldier was wounded; it's possible he was sent home to recuperate.

MILITARY RECORDS CHECKLIST

Use this worksheet to identify what military conflicts your ancestors may have fought in—and to track them once they've been found.

Ancestor name and life dates	Colonial Wars	American Revolution (1775-1783)	1784-1811	War of 1812 (1812-1815)	Indian Wars (1815-1858)	Patriot War (1838)	Mexican War (1846-1848)	Civil War (1861-1865)	1866-1898	Spanish-American War (1898-1899)	Philippine Insurrection (1899-1902)	World War I (1917-1918)	World War II (1941-1945)

MILITARY DRAFT RECORDS WORKSHEET

Use this form to organize information that can help you in your search for an ancestor's military draft registration. If you're not sure of a detail, leave it blank or provide your best guess(es) based on research you've done. Update the information as you discover more.

ANCESTOR INFORMATION

Name	
Birth date/approximate year	
Birthplace	
State(s) and county(ies) where he resided before and during the war	
Occupation(s)	
Parents' names	
Name of first/only spouse	
Marriage date and place	
Names of other spouses	
Marriage date(s) and place(s)	

MILITARY DRAFT ELIGIBILITY

For which war(s) was this ancestor eligible to be registered for the draft?	☐ Civil War (men born about 1811-1848) ☐ World War I (men born about 1872-1900) ☐ World War II (men born about 1877-1925)
If Civil War, was state Union or Confederate?	
How old was this ancestor when war began or US entered war? (Civil War began 1861; World War I entered 1917; World War II entered 1941)	
Have you found any indication that this ancestor actually served in the war?	
If so, what and where found?	

DRAFT RECORDS SEARCH TRACKER

Collection name	Search terms used	Date searched

NOTES

MILITARY PENSION RECORDS WORKSHEET

Use this form to organize information that can help you in your search for an ancestor's military pension record. If you're not sure of a detail, leave it blank or provide your best guess(es) based on research you've done. Update the information as you uncover new records.

ANCESTOR INFORMATION

Name	
Birth date/approximate year	
State(s) and county(ies) where he resided before war	
State(s) and county(ies) where he resided after war	
Date and place of death	
Cemetery where buried	
Name of first/only spouse	
Name of second spouse	
If spouse was a widow who then re-married, what was her new surname?	

MILITARY SERVICE INFORMATION

Name		
War		If Civil War, Union of Confederate?
Type of service	☐ US Army ☐ US Navy ☐ colonial militia ☐ state militia ☐ other	
Unit name/number (if known)		
Rank (if known)		
Commanding officer's name (if known)		
What indications of service have you found?	☐ family history or lore ☐ online index ☐ published roster or muster roll ☐ bounty land record ☐ service record ☐ 1890 veterans census ☐ draft registration (Civil War)	☐ lineage society database ☐ pension voucher or list ☐ tombstone marker ☐ soldiers' home records ☐ county history ☐ other

PENSION RECORDS SEARCH TRACKER

Collection name	Search terms used	Date searched

NOTES

5

IMMIGRATION RECORDS

Immigration to America was scattered throughout the decades up until the early twentieth century. At that time, the "great wave" of immigrants from around the world came ashore—mostly at New York.

The first "immigrants"—colonists—arrived in 1607 and established the Jamestown settlement in Virginia. The New World continued to be colonized by immigrants from various ethnic backgrounds, including English, Dutch, Spanish, Irish, German, and French.

World events had a significant impact on immigration. For example, the Irish Potato Famine drove more than 750,000 Irish to America, and the discovery of gold in California in 1848 resulted in another large influx of immigrants from Latin America, China, Australia, and Europe. Whether coming over land from the East, via the Isthmus of Panama, or 'round the Horn, immigrants from across the Western Hemisphere flocked to San Francisco, a major port for debarkation and a jumping-off place for gold-seekers.

The turn of the twentieth century witnessed a huge population explosion of Italians, Greeks, and Catholics, as well as Jews escaping the pogroms of Eastern Europe. Areas heavily settled by immigrants were the Midwest (Germans, Swedes, and Norwegians), large cities like New York and Chicago (Italians, Irishmen, Jews), and New England (Canadians).

Well-known immigration stations included New York's Castle Garden (1820–1892) and Ellis Island (1892–1954), which served as the ports of entry for millions of immigrants along the East Coast, welcoming huge steamships (such as the *SS Abyssinia*) that brought scores of immigrants to the United States from Europe (image **A**).

A

Large steamships such as the *US Abyssinia* carried millions of immigrants to the United States in the late nineteenth and early-twentieth centuries.

B

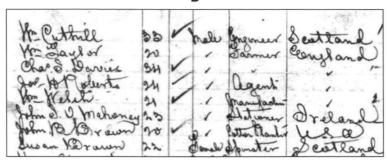

Immigrant ancestors, along with their ages, places of origin, and other information, are listed in passenger lists at major ports like New York City.

Although immigration stations were located around the country, New York was the first American stop for millions of immigrants. Unsurprisingly, the largest Ancestry.com immigration collection includes more than 82 million records of New York passenger lists.

The Ancestry.com collections related to Immigration and Travel include the following subcategories:
- Passenger Lists
- Citizenship & Naturalization Records
- Border Crossings & Passports
- Crew Lists
- Immigration & Emigration Books
- Ship Pictures & Descriptions

PASSENGER LISTS

Passenger lists are the primary source of information on immigrant ancestors (image **B**). Depending on the year and port, passenger lists can log immigrants' names, ages, home countries, marital statuses, and more, providing valuable information for researchers.

Although the primary "New York Passenger List" collection spans the years from 1820 to 1954, don't despair if your ancestors arrived before 1820; this collection actually has records dating back to Colonial times, including "The Original Scots Colonists of Early America, 1612–1783" and "The Pioneers of Massachusetts, 1620–1650." If you have a broad idea of the year your ancestor immigrated, attack this collection by filtering by date.

See the Passenger List Search Worksheet at the end of the chapter for help transcribing these records.

CITIZENSHIP & NATURALIZATION RECORDS

These collections are another hodgepodge group of records, including indexes, original documents, and even Native American enrollment records. Immigrants could become citizens through naturalization, first by completing a Declaration of Intention (some of which can be found in this category). If you have no idea when (or even *if*) your ancestor applied for citizenship or naturalization, search across the entire collection while filtering for location, then approximate date. When searching these collections, don't forget to look at federal census records from 1900 to 1930, as they have questions about citizenship.

See the Naturalization Record Extraction Worksheet at the end of the chapter for help transcribing these records.

BORDER CROSSINGS & PASSPORTS

Although we tend to think about immigration in terms of ships coming into New York, many people entered the United States via Canada. As Ancestry.com notes, it was often cheaper to book passage to Canada, then enter the United States from the north.

As a result, ancestors who crossed the border rather than arrived along the East Coast may appear in bordercrossing records, found in this category on Ancestry.com. Sadly, records of Canada-US border crossings weren't kept until 1895. Similarly, if you're looking for ancestors who entered the United States via Mexico, you'll find records from as early as 1903.

Passports are another helpful kind of resource and some of the most interesting resources in this particular collection. When William F. Cody (Buffalo Bill) took his famous Wild West Show to Europe, he filled out a passport application. As you can see in image **C**, Bill, at 6'1" according to his passport application, must have towered over his contemporaries, as the average height for a male in 1900 was 5'6".

C

OATH OF ALLEGIANCE. *William Frederick Cody*

Further I do solemnly swear that I will support and defend the Constitution of the United States against all enemies, foreign and domestic; that I will bear true faith and allegiance to the same; and that I take this obligation freely, without any mental reservation or purpose of evasion: So HELP ME GOD.

Sworn to before me, this **2d** *day)*
of **Jany** *____ 190 6 ;*

A. L. Scantlebury #214

Notary Public Kings County.   *Notary Public.*

Certificate filed in New York County. DESCRIPTION OF APPLICANT.

Age, *59* years.   Mouth, *Medium*
Stature, *6* feet *1* inches, Eng.   Chin, *square*
Forehead, *high*   Hair, *grey*
Eyes, *brown*   Complexion, *florid*
Nose, *straight*   Face, *oval*

Passport applications can provide unique details, such as the applicant's height.

If your ancestors traveled abroad, you can find amazing detail in their passport applications, which asked for proof of citizenship. Interestingly, though, Americans didn't always need a passport. Although required during the Civil War and World War I, American travelers weren't required to have one until 1941. (For more information on the history of passports <www.archives.gov/research/passport>.)

For both border crossings and passports, begin with a name search, then filter to approximate date and location.

CREW LISTS

These comprise a twentieth-century collection of seamen who worked on seafaring vessels, although some collections have both passengers and crew names. Start here with a name-based search; if that proves fruitless, search by ship name.

IMMIGRATION & EMIGRATION BOOKS

This subcategory contains an interesting blend of both true immigration records and records that mention immigration peripherally. For example, this subcategory houses a collection of records from the Emigrant Savings Bank in New York. This bank was established in 1850 to serve Irish immigrants who came to America during the Potato Famine, and the collection has an index to the bank's records and also an image linked to where more information (such as place of birth, occupation, and names of relatives) may be found.

Several items in this subcategory are digitized books, so your ancestor's name may not appear in search results if there's any kind of name variance between how you searched and how the name appears in an index. Be sure to browse the book's index (if available) to double-check for possible name varia-

D

The Original Scots Colonists of Early America, 1612-1783

1. Abbott, Frederick, Jacobite, tr. 29 June 1716, fr. Liverpool to Jamaica or Va, in *Elizabeth & Anne.* (SPC.1716.310)
2. Abercrombie, Bobby, b. 1753, servant, res. Dysart Fife, sh. May 1775, fr. Leith to Philadelphia, in *Friendship.* (PRO.T47.12)
3. Abercromby, John, Jacobite, res. Skeith Banffshire, tr. 29 June 1716, fr. Liverpool to Jamaica or Va, in *Elizabeth & Anne.* (SPC.1716.310)
4. Abernethy, Janet, thief, res. Foveran Aberdeenshire, pts. William Abernethy, tr. 1772, in *Betsy*, arr. James River Va 29 Apr 1772. (SRO.JC27.10.3)
5. Adair, John, b. 1730, laborer, res. Beak, sh. 31 May 1775, fr. Stranraer to N.Y., in *Jackie*, m. Janet McNillie, ch. Janet Jean Agnes John. (PRO.T47.12)

Books about immigration to the United States, such as this digitized book on Scots in Colonial America, can feature information about your ancestors.

tions. Image **D** from the digitized book *The Original Scots Colonists of Early America, 1612–1783* gives you an idea of what kind of information you might expect to find.

Note: Apparently people weren't shy about "naming names," as you can see with Janet Abernethy's occupation ("thief").

SHIP PICTURES & DESCRIPTIONS

As the name suggests, this is the subcategory to search for an actual picture of your ancestor's ship. This group only contains three collections, for a total of a little more than three million records. Remember, there's information about early ships without a photo or a drawing, but you can still discover a lot of information by reading a ship's description. If you find a ship of interest, be sure to note details such as number of funnels or masts, as you can probably find a drawing of a similar type of vessel.

Immigration Clues in Census Records

Census records can also provide information on your ancestor's immigration. Once you've exhausted the Immigration & Travel collections, go back to chapter 2 and review the columns in the census records related to immigration and naturalization. In addition, remember that censuses indicate a person's state or country of birth beginning in 1850.

1900 census clues
- What year did the person immigrate to the United States?
- How many years has the person been in the United States?
- Is the person naturalized?

1910 census clues
- What year did the person immigrate to the United States?
- Is the person naturalized or an alien?
- Can the person speak English? If not, what language does the person speak?

1920 census clues
- What year did the person immigrate to the United States?
- Is the person naturalized or an alien?
- If naturalized, what was the year of naturalization?

1930 census clues
- What year did the person immigrate to the United States? Is the person naturalized or an alien?
- Is the person able to speak English?

1940 census clues
- What is the person's place of birth? If foreign born, is the person a citizen?

Abbreviations for the 1900, 1910, 1920, and 1930 census questions about naturalization are *Al* for alien, *Pa* for "first papers," and *Na* for naturalized.

Look, too, in the 1870 census for the "Male Citizens of the U.S. of 21 years of age and upwards" column. If the person was a foreign-born citizen, this means that he was naturalized by the year 1870. This census year also has checkmarks if the person's parents were of foreign birth.

Also check the 1880 and 1900 through 1940 censuses, as these contained questions about the respondent's parents' place of birth.

MOTHER TONGUE (OR NATIVE LANGUAGE) OF FOREIGN BORN				CITIZENSHIP	
Language spoken in home before coming to the United States	CODE (For office use only. Do not write in these columns)			Year of immigration to the United States	Naturalization
	State or M. T.	Country	Nativity		
21	A	B	C	22	23
French	12	12	V	1913 Ac	
French	12	12	V	1905 Ac	
	53	42	0		
English	00	04	V	1927 Al	
	56	13	0		

Census records often include information that you can use when researching for ancestors' immigration records.

RESEARCH GOAL: *Find any immigration records for Friedrich Schor (Shore), who arrived in America from Switzerland in the 1700s.*

STEP ❶ Search for a collection.
Go to the Card Catalog and filter for Immigration & Travel > Passenger Lists. Next, filter for USA and 1700s. I did not filter for any particular state because I have no idea of the arrival port city.

STEP ❷ Select your collection.
This filtering led to forty-two possible collections. I started with the one with the largest number of records (more than five million): "U.S. and Canada, Passenger and Immigration Lists Index, 1500s–1900s."

STEP ❸ Enter your search terms.
Because of the spelling of Friedrich Schor (Frederick Shore) and my uncertainty about any dates, I only filled out the Last Name and Birth Year fields.

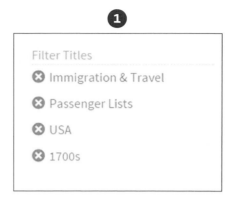

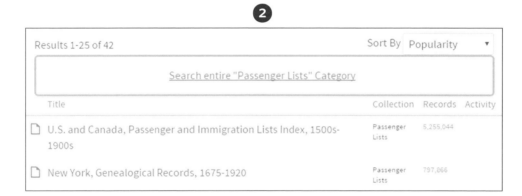

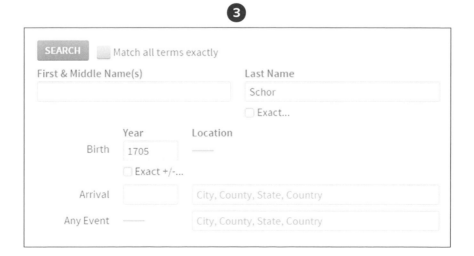

STEP ④ View your results and compare to prior research.

This search returned twenty-five results, the first being "Frid Schor." By hovering my mouse above Frid, I could see a box with all of the information about this immigrant.

Talk about luck! The record matched my own previous research, which had Frid's wife as Margaretha and his first three children as Friedrich, Henrich, Michael, and Johannes. My assumption is that Michael either didn't travel with his parent or that he died in childhood. Not only do I have information about the arrival place (Carolina or Pennsylvania), I also have the source from which the information was extracted.

Because my search resulted in only twenty-five people, I ran through all of them and found other family matches. In going through other matches, it appears that this Friedrich arrived in Philadelphia, not Carolina.

NAME:	Frid Schor
BIRTH YEAR:	1706
ARRIVAL YEAR:	1750
ARRIVAL PLACE:	Carolina or Pennsylvania
AGE:	44
FAMILY MEMBERS:	Wife Margreth Schneider; Child Fridrich; Child Heinrich; Child Johannes; Child Margreth
SOURCE PUBLICATION CODE:	1960
PRIMARY IMMIGRANT:	Schor, Frid
ANNOTATION:	Contains lists of emigrants from the Cantons of Bern and Basel, 1709-1795, taken from the official archives of those cities. Items nos. 1952 and 1960, with Leo Schelbert's "Notes on Lists of Swiss Emigrants" from item no. 8040, pp. 245-255, are all in the
SOURCE BIBLIOGRAPHY:	FAUST, ALBERT BERNHARDT, AND GAIUS MARCUS BRUMBAUGH. Lists of Swiss Emigrants in the Eighteenth Century to the American Colonies. Vol. 2. Washington, D.C.: The National Genealogical Society, 1925. Reprinted by Genealogical Publishing Co., Baltimore, 1976. ix, 243p.
PAGE:	159

EXERCISE ② Finding Canadian Bordercrossing Records

RESEARCH GOAL: *Find Canadian bordercrossing records for Joseph or Anna (Anne) Brooks (both born around 1860), knowing they had a child Joseph Edward born in 1889 in Illinois, and so they immigrated sometime between their 1882 marriage in Canada and the 1889 birth of their child.*

STEP ❶ Find your collection and enter search terms.

Go to the Card Catalog and choose the category Immigration & Travel > Border Crossings & Passports, using filters as necessary. In this case, I filtered for the 1880s as the decade. This left only seven collections to search, none of which seemed relevant to my research goal.

Note that the "Canadian Immigrant Records" collection is for people going to Canada, not coming from Canada.

STEP ❷ Adjust filters as necessary.

When I removed the 1880s filter, the search returned twenty-seven collections; unfortunately the best one, "U.S., Border Crossings from Canada to U.S., 1895–1956," didn't have records from the correct time period.

❶

📄	U.S. Passport Applications, 1795-1925
📄	Canadian Immigrant Records, Part One
📄	Pomerania, Germany, Passenger Lists, 1869-1901 (in German)
📄	Lithuania, Internal Passports, 1919-1940
📄	Connecticut, Passport and Birth Certificates, 1852-1928
📄	Israel, Index to Records from U.S. Consular Posts in Jerusalem, Jaffa, and Haifa, 1857-1935
📄	Web: Denmark, Emigration Index, 1868-1908

❷

Results 1-25 of 27   Sort By | Popularity ▾

Search entire "Border Crossings & Passports" Category

Title	Collection	Records	Activity
📄 U.S., Border Crossings from Canada to U.S., 1895-1956	Border Crossings & Passports	5,356,153	
📄 U.S. Passport Applications, 1795-1925	Border Crossings & Passports	1,835,566	
📄 Border Crossings: From Mexico to U.S., 1895-1964	Border Crossings & Passports	5,807,437	
📄 Border Crossings: From U.S. to Canada, 1908-1935	Border Crossings & Passports	1,640,346	

STEP ❸ Refine your search.

Add additional details (such as keywords) or redo your filters. Because their son was born in Chicago, I added *Illinois* as a keyword, but these results were also unhelpful.

I tried a search with new filters. This resulted in fourteen collections. I selected "U.S. and Canada, Passenger and Immigration Lists Index, 1500s–1900s," hoping to find the family in a list of people going to Canada.

STEP ❹ Search broadly when all else fails.

I searched the entire Immigration & Travel category, but (again) had too many results and not enough information to narrow down to the family for which I was searching.

Unfortunately, I had to abandon this particular search, as Brooks is too common a name to narrow down search results. I simply don't know enough about this family to know if I'm looking at the right Brooks.

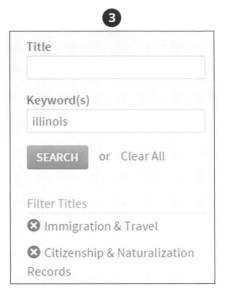

❸

Title

Keyword(s)

illinois

SEARCH   or   Clear All

Filter Titles

❌ Immigration & Travel

❌ Citizenship & Naturalization Records

❹

Title	Collection	Records	Activity
Results 1-25 of 501		Sort By	Popularity ▼
Search entire "Immigration & Travel" Category			
New York, Passenger Lists, 1820-1957	Immigration & Travel	82,920,850	
U.S. Naturalization Record Indexes, 1791-1992 (Indexed in World Archives Project)	Immigration & Travel	5,823,355	
UK, Outward Passenger Lists, 1890-1960	Immigration & Travel	23,768,544	

STEP ❺ Look for other resources.

What would I do next? Turn to other resources such as newspapers, books, membership directories, and city directories. Any mention I can find of this family, particularly one with the year noted, will help me go back to the immigration collections with more information with which to filter.

❺

NEWPORT BEACH (1918) CITY DIRECTORY   53

Buck Melvin S prop Bungalow Court h Central av nr B, Balboa
Buckingham Emma A Mrs h ss Bay av 2 w of Lindo av, E Newport
Bullis Rowena r Buena Vista cor Alvarado, Balboa
Bullis Sherman (Elizabeth) summer res h Buena Vista cor Alvarado, Balboa
Bungalow Court Apartments Melvin S Buck prop Central av nr B, Balboa
Bunch Frank mgr Balboa Market
Burnham Wm H summer res h Bay Island, E Newport
Burns Colgan W (Jessie) summer res h Ocean av 4 w of 24th, Newport Beach
Burns Henry J (Ida H) ice cream and lunches Main cor Central av h Surf av cor Washington, Balboa
Burns Ida M r Surf av cor Washington, Balboa
Butler Chas O (Blanche B) bldg contr P O Balboa
Butterfield Chauncey C (Mary) cottages for rent h Butterfield pl cor 20th, Newport Beach
Byerly Saml summer res h Diamond av, Balboa Island

EXERCISE ③ Finding Naturalization Papers

RESEARCH GOAL: *Search Ancestry.com for naturalization records for Nicholas Preovolos, born about 1895 in Greece.*

STEP ❶ Search for collections.

Go to the Card Catalog and select the category Immigration & Travel > Citizenship & Naturalization Records. Filter with USA and 1900s. (Since Nicholas was born in 1895 and survived to adulthood, I knew I wouldn't find a naturalization record pre-1900.)

STEP ❷ Select the collection with the best chance of giving your results, then enter your search terms.

I wasn't sure which collection might give me the best chance of success, so I selected the one with the largest number of records: "U.S. Naturalization Record Indexes, 1791–1992 (Indexed in World Archives Project)."

Guess, what? No results. My second choice was "Selected U.S. Naturalization Records—Original Documents, 1790–1974." Using the same search criteria, I still no results.

STEP ❸ Search the whole category.

At this point I decided to do a global search of all collections in the Citizenship & Naturalization Records category.

Oh-oh. This time the search gave me results—coincidentally, in the same collection I searched in Step 1 *that gave me zero results*! Searching the entire category gave me the results I needed that displayed a thumbnail overview of the record and an image of the original records themselves.

I went back and re-searched the collection "Selected U.S. Naturalization Records—Original Documents, 1790–1974," just in case I missed something the first time around. (I didn't.) For some reason, the Preovolos records didn't show up in this collection when it was searched alone, but they did appear when I did a global search! My only explanation is a tiny glitch in the search engine for that particular collection. But my lesson was learned: Approach the problem from as many directions as possible, and if you don't find something in a solitary collection, go back and do a category-wide search.

①

②

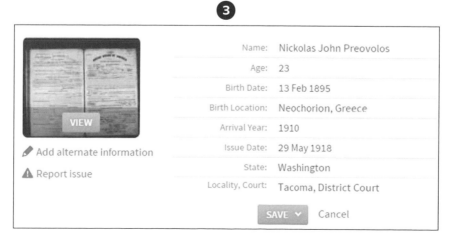

③

EXERCISE ④ Finding a Person of Interest in Immigration Records

RESEARCH GOAL: *Find my uncle's father, who immigrated to the United States from Norway, in some kind of immigration record.*

STEP ❶ Search the category.

Select Immigration & Travel from the main menu and enter the information in the search boxes. In this case, all I knew was the name: Perry (Pers) Hjetland.

STEP ❷ Evaluate results.

Unfortunately the immigration list was an index only, which pointed me to a printed book—something for further research. The second result, while only an index, did give me a naturalization date.

STEP ❸ Look for more resources.

Because the book (per the Ancestry.com Annotation field) contained "Date and place of declaration of intent, or date and place of immigration...birth date and place, physical characteristics, location of emigration, residence, family data, and other information," my next step would be to contact the repository (Northwest Missouri Genealogical Society, listed under Source Bibliography) and ask someone to do a lookup for me.

STEP ❹ View suggested records.

Remember how Ancestry.com provides a list of suggested collections relative to your search? In this case I went to the suggested "1925 Kansas State Census," which gave me Perry's birthdate and the names of his wife and children.

❶

SEARCH	☐ Match all terms exactly

First & Middle Name(s)

perry

Last Name

hjetland

☐ Exact...   ☐ Exact...

	Day	Month	Year	Location
Birth	—	—	☐	City, County, State, Count

❷

📄 **U.S. and Canada, Passenger and Immigration Lists Index, 1500s-1900s**
PASSENGER LISTS

NAME: **Perry Hjetland**
BIRTH: abt 1881
ARRIVAL: 1904 - Kansas

📄 **Missouri, Western District Naturalization Index, 1848-1990**
CITIZENSHIP & NATURALIZATION RECORDS

NAME: **Perry O Hjetland**
CIVIL: 4 Nov 1908

View Image

3

No Image
Text-only collection

🖊 Add alternate information

⚠ Report issue

Name:	Perry Hjetland
Birth Year:	abt 1881
Arrival Year:	1904
Arrival Place:	Kansas
Age:	23
Source Publication Code:	1174.35
Primary Immigrant:	Hjetland, Perry
Annotation:	Date and place of declaration of intent, or date and place of immigration. Birth date and place, physical characteristics, location of emigration, residence, family data, and other information provided.
Source Bibliography:	CITIZENSHIP RECORDS OF IMMIGRANTS IN DONIPHAN COUNTY, KANSAS. St. Joseph, MO: Northwest Missouri Genealogical Society, n.d. 59p.
Page:	23

SAVE ⌄   Cancel

4

Suggested Records ❓

📄 Kansas State Census Collection, 1855-1925
Perry O Hjetland

📄 1940 United States Federal Census
Perry O Hjetland

📄 1920 United States Federal Census
Perry O Hjetland

📄 1930 United States Federal Census
Perry O Hjetland

📄 1910 United States Federal Census
Perry Hietland

➤ Select a primary goal before you begin searching—e.g., finding your ancestor's place of origin or the date of arrival in America.

➤ Have a fairly close estimate of your ancestor's immigration entry point. There's no point in searching New York passenger lists if your family immigrated through Charleston!

➤ Be creative in spelling names. Remember in the example earlier in this chapter that Friedrich Schor (Frederick Shore) showed up on a passenger list as *Frid*.

➤ Listen to family stories. While not always accurate, the tale about your great-great-grandpa coming to America from LeHavre, France, may help you find a departure list.

➤ Consider searching lists of immigrants into Canada. Many immigrants arrived in Canada, then crossed to the United States along the border.

➤ Search for ancestors in the years surrounding your time frame if you can't find them. Circumstances may have caused family members to immigrate at different times or leave and re-enter the country. For example, men often came to America, got a job, and settled down for a year or two before their wives and children arrived.

➤ Find your ancestors' extended family and neighbors. Immigrants often traveled with friends or family, settling in the same town or area. If you can't find your ancestor, use census records to look for friends or relatives who might have joined your ancestor in his travels or who settled down next to him.

➤ Learn about your ancestor's place of origin. In Schor's case, the records note he came from the Cantons of Bern and Basel (Switzerland) in 1750. Having that information, I searched the history of those places at that time to see if I could find a clue of why he and his family left Switzerland for America.

ANCESTRAL VILLAGE WORKSHEET

One of the first steps to finding an immigrant ancestor is learning about his ancestral village in the old country. Use this worksheet to track information about your ancestor's town.

Town/village name (in English)	
Names in other applicable languages	
Other historical names (note years of use)	
Geographic coordinates (if known)	
Local government website/contact info	
Date established and years ancestors lived there	
Primary language(s) (note years if applicable)	
Primary religion(s) (note years if applicable)	
Modern county, state, country, etc.	
Historical kingdom, province, state, county, duchy, etc.	
Church parishes the town belonged to	
Governmental seat for the town's region	
Major geological features (river, mountains, etc.)	
Timeline: Note changes in governing authority, boundary changes, major events, etc.	
Gazetteer/other sources used (include page numbers)	

PASSENGER LIST SEARCH WORKSHEET

Use this form to organize information that can help you in your search for an immigrant ancestor's passenger list. If you're not sure of a detail, leave it blank or provide your best guess(es) based on research you've done. Update the information as you uncover new records.

Immigrant information

Original name: _____

Spelling variants/other names used: _____

Birth date: _____ Birthplace: _____ Occupation: _____

Immigrant's family

Spouse: _____ Marriage date and place: _____

Children

Name	Date of birth	Place of birth

Migration information

Estimated departure date: _____ From which country or region?: _____

Possible departure ports: _____

Ship name: _____ Estimated arrival date: _____

Possible arrival ports: _____

Possible traveling companions

Name	Sex	Age	Relationship

PASSENGER LISTS SEARCH TRACKER

Collection name	Search terms used	Date searched

NOTES

NATURALIZATION RECORD EXTRACTION WORKSHEET

If your immigrant ancestors became citizens, their naturalization records can reveal important clues about their lives in the old country. Immigration generally followed a two-step process. Immigrants first filed a Declaration of Intention proclaiming their desire to become a citizen. Then, after fulfilling the requirements, they had to file a Petition for Naturalization to have their citizenship granted. Immigrants could file at any court they chose (local, state or federal). In 1906, the US government standardized naturalization forms. This worksheet is based on that standardized Petition for Naturalization and Declaration of Intention; earlier documents may not contain all the information here. Extract the information you find in Ancestry.com's collections of records here.

PETITION OF NATURALIZATION

Court	
Petitioner's name	
Residence	
Occupation	
Birth date	
Birthplace	
Port of departure	
Date of emigration	
Port of arrival	
Vessel	
Date, place, and court where declaration was filed	
Marital status	
Spouse's name	
Spouse's birthdate and place	
Spouse's residence	
Children's names, birth dates, birthplaces, and residences	
Former citizenship	
Date when US residence commenced	
Time of residence in state	
Date of petition	
Personal description	
Name changes	
Other information listed in record	

DECLARATION OF INTENTION

Court	
Applicant's name	
Applicant's age	
Occupation	
Personal description	
Birth date	
Birthplace	
Present address	
Port of departure	
Vessel	
Last foreign residence	
Marital status	
Spouse's name	
Spouse's birthdate and place	
Citizenship	
Port of arrival	
Date of arrival	
Date of application	
Other information listed in record	

6

HISTORICAL MAPS, IMAGES, NEWSPAPERS, AND PUBLICATIONS

Although historical maps, images, and other publications may seem an odd grouping of collections, they all serve a single purpose: adding details to genealogy basics like names, dates, and places.

When you're researching your family tree, the timeline may show that an ancestor was living in 1860, but do you have any way of knowing whether he leaned towards Abraham Lincoln, Stephen Douglas, John C. Breckinridge, or John Bell? Of course, you'll never know for certain, but it's possible that newspaper articles or genealogy books can give you an inkling of the county's political makeup.

And while the odds are against you finding a photo of your ancestor in a collection, I can almost guarantee you'll find pictures of places, people, and things he would have seen, known, or used in everyday life, like a soap powder ad from the 1880s (image **A**).

Remember, too, the first photograph wasn't taken until the 1820s, but that doesn't mean you can't find an artistic rendition of a family farmhouse or a famous person like General Francis Marion, the Revolutionary War's "Swamp Fox" (image **B**).

Contemporary publications, such as newspapers, can also aid your research. Of course, finding an obituary can open avenues of research, particularly

A

Historical images, such as this advertisement for soap powder, give glimpses of everyday life during your ancestor's time.

B

Even if you don't find images of your ancestors, historical portraits, like this one of a Revolutionary War general, can give you a sense for your ancestors' times.

those obits that name children, place of birth, cause of death, place of burial, and religious affiliation. But newspapers can also provide contextual information about your ancestor's community: the town's latest gossip, big news stories of the day, and what was important to his town's citizens.

I have to admit, though, of all the collections, my favorite is "Maps, Atlases & Gazetteers"—I've always been a map geek. In our world of GPS navigation, we can easily forget the value of a printed map. But for genealogists, maps are an invaluable resource, giving us a visual representation of ancestral migrations and homestead locations and even helping us determine which county you're likely to find family records in.

Let's look at this broad grouping of collections and see what's available.

MAPS, ATLASES & GAZETTEERS

There are roughly two hundred collections of maps, atlases, and gazetteers in this group, more than eighty of which relate to the United States and more than ninety to Europe. And in case you're wondering about the difference between the three:

- **Maps** show the physical terrain of an area and generally include boundary lines. When searching maps, you'll primarily be looking for place names in a smaller locality (such as a township or county) rather than ancestor names.

- **Atlases** are organized collections of maps. When searching atlases, you're looking either for more detailed maps of specific places or researching a larger area, such as a state, country, or even continent.

- **Gazetteers** are detailed listings of references to and resources about localized geographic locations, including demographics, statistics, and physical features like the elevation of mountains. While gazetteers can include maps, they generally are text-heavy and provide detailed information about the layout and composition of an area. Gazetteers are especially helpful when researching foreign localities, as they can help you sift through tricky place-name changes.

My very favorite collection in the Maps category is "U.S., Indexed County Land Ownership Maps, 1860–1918," which contains close to seven million records.

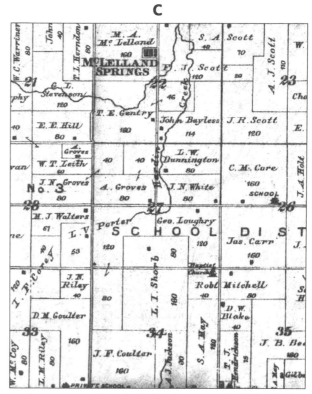

Land maps can provide such detail as the names of individual land owners and their neighbors.

If you've never done land research, you're in for a treat; this collection contains approximately twelve hundred US county land ownership atlases from the Library of Congress.

Here's how these atlases work: While some maps show detailed boundary lines and others are sketches, they also show the names of every landowner at the time the atlas was compiled. If you're wondering "so what?" the answer is simple: Families lived next to or close to one another, so if you find one ancestor on a land map, you'll probably find another.

Image **C** is a detail from an 1895 land map of Cass County, Missouri. It shows the names of landowners, the boundaries of their properties and the number of acres owned. (If you need help understanding how land was divided, check out the Bureau of Land Management General Land Office website <www.blm.gov>.)

Items in the Map category date from 1513 ("U.S. Maps Collection") to recent times. Don't you think it would be fascinating to see what the world looked like according to your 1650 ancestor? Bet you didn't realize California was an island, did you? (Confused? See image **D**.)

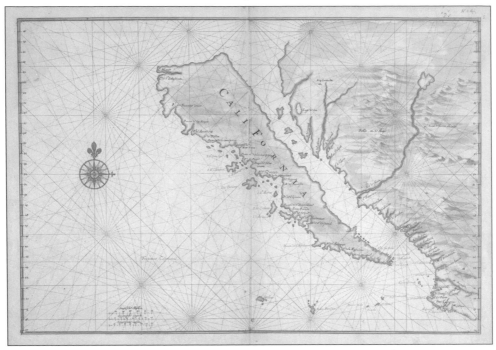

Historical maps can be enlightening, even if we know now that they're not geographically accurate.

E

NEWSPAPERS.

In the spring of 1836 John King purchased at Cincinnati, Ohio, and brought to Dubuque, a Smith press with the necessary type, and published the Dubuque *Visitor*. William Cary Jones was foreman of the office at a salary of $350.00 a year and boarding. Andrew Keesicker was compositor. In 1842 this press and type were taken to Lancaster, Wisconsin, and on it was printed the Grant County *Herald*. Subsequently the same press was taken to St. Paul, Minnesota, and from it was issued the first paper printed in Minnesota Territory, called the St. Paul *Pioneer*. In 1858 the same press was taken to Sioux Falls, in Dakota Territory, whereon to print the first newspaper published in that Territory, called the Dakota *Democrat*. In March, 1862, the Sioux Indians burned the town of Sioux Falls, and this pioneer of American civilization perished in the flames. From this beginning grew the press of Iowa as found to-day. Of the 643 papers issued in the State, 41 are issued daily, 1 tri-weekly, 9 semi-weekly, 548 weekly, 1 bi-weekly, 7 semi-monthly, 34 monthly, and 2 bi-monthly. 306 cities and villages have papers issued in them.

Gazetteers can sometimes include detailed information about local businesses, such as this history of the newspaper industry in Iowa.

As much as I love maps, I wouldn't want you to search them to the exclusion of the other two sources. In particular, don't neglect searching through gazetteers. As mentioned earlier, gazetteers contain important information on the local economy, businesses, and demographics. For example, gazetteers often include business directories with articles like this one in the "Iowa Gazetteer and Business Directory, 1884–1885" (image **E**).

NEWSPAPERS & PUBLICATIONS

These eclectic collections span historical printed material, from catalogues to newspapers to magazines. It's possible you'll find details about your ancestors: their town, neighbors, and local events. I'm sure you already know the value of an historical obituary, but did you realize you could take a peek at the Sears, Roebuck and Co., spring catalog from 1900? Check out the Ladies' Acme Jewel Bicycle for $13.75, with wheels available in custom colors of green, maroon, or black (image **F**).

Newspapers

The Big Daddy of this category is the "U.S. Obituary Collection, 1930–2015" collection, featuring nearly 35 million names. The records in this collection have been

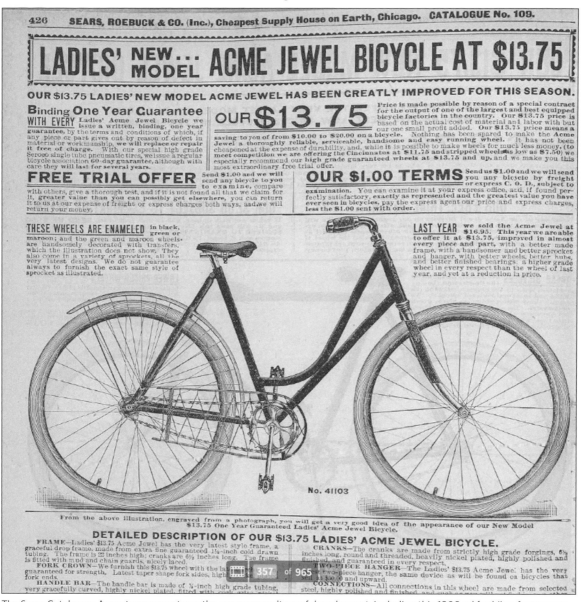

The Sears Catalog on Ancestry.com captures the consumer culture of decades past, including this 1900 ad for bikes for women.

extracted from obituaries to include the most relevant genealogical information, as you can see in image **G**.

The second- and third-largest US collections in Newspapers are "Associated Press, Name Card Index to AP Stories, 1905–1990" (2 million) and "Historical Newspapers, Birth, Marriage, & Death Announcements, 1851–2003" (1.5 million). When searching the AP Index, be sure to scroll to the bottom of the search form page, as there are instructions on how to read an article *after* you find an index card.

See the worksheets at the end of this chapter for help recording obituaries and other newspaper clippings about your ancestors.

Unfortunately, the collection of historical newspapers only contains items from a select group of publications:

- *New York Times* (1851–2003)
- *Los Angeles Times* (1881–1985)
- *Boston Globe* (1872–1923)
- *Chicago Defender* (Big Weekend and National Editions) (1921–1975)
- *Chicago Tribune* (1850–1985)
- *Hartford Courant* (1791–1942)
- *Washington Post* (1877–1990)
- *Atlanta Constitution* (1869–1929)

Name of Deceased:	Virgil Thomas Faulkenberry
Gender:	Male
Birth Date:	30 Sep 1928
Birth Place:	Ellington, Reynolds, Missouri, USA
Death Place:	Virginia Beach, Princess Anne, Virginia, USA
Obituary Date:	22 Sep 2013
Spouse's Name:	Anna
Parents' Names:	Lillie
Childrens' Names:	Lauralynn and husband Mike, James and wife Cyndi, Richard and wife Jennifer, Kathryn and husband Andy, Tani and husband Stan and Jennifer
Siblings' Names:	Billy Joe; Ed, Paul, Jr, Jimmy; Paulette; Winnie

Records from Ancestry.com's massive collection of obituaries include only the most relevant genealogical information.

PERIODICALS & MAGAZINES

If your ancestors lived in Virginia or Pennsylvania, you're in luck—this subcategory has several issues of *Genealogies of Virginia Families from the William and Mary College Quarterly* and *Genealogies of Pennsylvania Families from the Pennsylvania Genealogical*

Magazine. Other similar publications are from Maine, North Carolina, and Oregon. These types of publications have articles that mention people by name and can often be a first occurrence of finding your family in early America.

If your family was mentioned in one of these genealogy quarterlies, what can you expect to find? You may discover records of burial in a family cemetery, ancestry information, marriage announcements, or church memberships. For example, image **H** (an excerpt from a genealogy quarterly) contains detailed information about one of my Ballard ancestors.

Another collection of particular interest to those with Quaker ancestors is "U.S., Quaker Periodicals, 1828–1929." Per Ancestry.com: "This database contains digitized volumes of more than sixty Quaker publications, including some foreign-language periodicals. Names have been indexed from a variety of articles including births, marriage notices, obituaries, officers, missionaries, committee members, names of people who have moved, and other references to members of the Society of Friends." Now that's a find.

HISTORICAL IMAGES

Historical images can be found across almost any category of Ancestry.com's Card Catalog. But for this chapter I'm going to concentrate on one category: Pictures.

With less than forty collections, Pictures is the smallest of the categories, but among its holdings are the 169 million records in "Public Member Photos &

H

Thomas Ballard b. 1630; buried March 24, 1689. Clerk of York County in 1652 and for many years later. Burgess from James City in 1666, member of the council in 1675, speaker of H. of B. in 1680. His case as a creditor of "Bacon the rebel" was in 1686 represented to the King by the council. Married Anne ——, who died Sept 26, 1678. William Thomas of York Co, whose wife was Anne ——, calls Ballard "son-in-law" and Sarah Henman and Jane Hillier wife of John Hillier, "daughters-in-law." Ballard's wife was captured by Bacon, and placed, with other ladies of the Council, upon his breastworks before Jamestown, where their white aprons warned Berkeley from attack. Capt Robert Baldrey [J. P., of York, came to Virginia in 1635, aged 18, and died in 1675] left his estate to the following children of Col. Ballard: John, eldest son, Thomas, Lydia, Elizabeth and Margaret. In 1694, Capt Thomas Ballard was sheriff of York Co and his brother, Francis (probably not born in 1675), sub-sheriff. John, I think, died without issue before 1694.

If you're lucky, you may find your ancestors mentioned in a published genealogy quarterly.

I

Results 1-25 of 39			Sort By	Popularity ▼

→ Search entire "Pictures" Category

Title	Collection	Records	Activity
📄 Public Member Photos & Scanned Documents	Pictures	191,047,126	
📄 U.S., School Yearbooks, 1880-2012	Pictures	372,489,557	UPDATED
📄 Private Member Photos	Pictures	69,713,602	
📄 Passenger Ships and Images	Pictures	3,965	
📄 Historic Catalogs of Sears, Roebuck and Co., 1896-1993	Pictures	252,502	

Unlike many other records categories, the Pictures category is often best searched all at once.

J

SEARCH   ☐ Match all terms exactly

First & Middle Name(s)

Last Name

	Year	Location
Birth		—
Lived In	—	City, County, State, Country
Any Event		City, County, State, Country

Keyword

"sni mills missouri"   ☑ Exact

e.g. pilot or "Flying Tigers" ⌄

Sometimes, searching with the Exact box checked (as I did in this search of the whole Pictures category) is your best option.

Scanned Documents." These are images that Ancestry.com users have uploaded themselves. Other large collections include yearbooks (see chapter 7 on social history), Civil War photos (see chapter 4 on military records), headstone photos (see chapter 3 on vital records), and passenger ships (see chapter 5 on immigration records).

This might be a case in which the quickest route to success is choosing the "Search entire 'Pictures' category" option (image **I**), since there's so much overlap in the images category that it's hard to know which collection your target might be sitting in.

For example, I wanted a photo of the tiny town of Sni Mills, Missouri. I honestly didn't have a clue of where to begin my search. Clicking on the search all link, I looked for *sni mills missouri* and checked the Exact box (image **J**).

Guess what? There were almost eighty results, with seventy of them coming from "Public Member Photos & Scanned Documents." Among them was a photo of the cemetery where I knew some family members were buried. Choosing to search the entire Pictures category rather than picking individual collections saved a lot of time.

EXERCISE ① Finding a Published Genealogy

RESEARCH GOAL: *Find information in a Virginia genealogies publication to learn more about the Ballard family.*

STEP ❶ Search for a collection.

Go to the Card Catalog and select the Newspapers & Publications category, then filter with USA, Periodicals & Magazines. This produced roughly forty results, so I added *Virginia* as a title word. This narrowed the number of collections down to six.

STEP ❷ Review your results and select your collection.

As you can see, volumes of *Genealogies of Virginia Families from the William and Mary College Quarterly* were categorized alphabetically. I selected Volume I, which covered names Adams to Clopton.

1

Title

virginia

Keyword(s)

SEARCH   or   Clear All

Filter Titles

❌ Newspapers & Publications

❌ Periodicals & Magazines

❌ USA

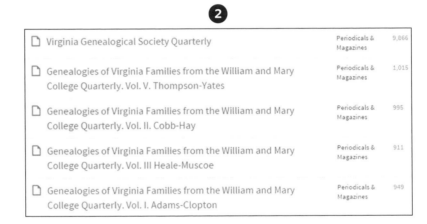

2

📄 Virginia Genealogical Society Quarterly	Periodicals & Magazines	9,866
📄 Genealogies of Virginia Families from the William and Mary College Quarterly. Vol. V. Thompson-Yates	Periodicals & Magazines	1,015
📄 Genealogies of Virginia Families from the William and Mary College Quarterly. Vol. II. Cobb-Hay	Periodicals & Magazines	995
📄 Genealogies of Virginia Families from the William and Mary College Quarterly. Vol. III Heale-Muscoe	Periodicals & Magazines	911
📄 Genealogies of Virginia Families from the William and Mary College Quarterly. Vol. I. Adams-Clopton	Periodicals & Magazines	949

STEP ❸ Enter your search terms.

I searched with the name of my ancestor (Thomas Ballard) and the year and county of his birth (**A**). This search returned fifteen results, but the one that interested me the most was taken from a chapter titled "Ballard Notes." The gold mine of information (**B**) was overwhelming and included family names, dates, places, events, and even included a generation of Ballards earlier than the one I knew about.

Will your search always be this lucky? No. But if you had ancestors who were early settlers in the original colonies, you have a much higher chance of success.

A

3

SEARCH   ☐ Match all terms exactly

First & Middle Name(s)   Last Name

Thomas   Ballard

☐ Exact...   ☐ Exact...

Year   Location

Any Event   1804   Albemarle County, Virginia, USA

☐ Exact +/-... ☐ Exact...

B

Thomas Ballard, son of Hon. Thomas and Anne (Thomas) Ballard, was burgess, justice of the peace, and Colonel of York county. His will was proved June 18, 1711. He married Katharine, daughter of John Huberd, and his issue was Anne, wife of John Major; Matthew, Elizabeth, Katharine, Thomas, Robert, John, William, and Mary, the last five, perhaps by a second wife, being under age. One of these, Captain John Ballard, of Yorktown (will proved in 1745), had Thomas, John, Robert, William, Catharine, Elizabeth, and Anne, and the last named, Robert, was clerk of Princess Anne county (York county Records). See Mr. James's note about the clerk of Princess Anne in the QUARTERLY, Vol. II., No. 2. The Ballard family is a very numerous one, and difficult to trace in later generations.

EXERCISE ② Finding and Analyzing Maps

RESEARCH GOAL: *Trace the route of the Brooks family to Highland Co., Ohio, circa 1800.*

STEP ❶ Find a collection to search based on what you know about your ancestors.

In a publication titled *A History of the Early Settlement of Highland County, Ohio,* I learned that my ancestor Benjamin Brooks emigrated with his grown children from Pennsylvania "down the Ohio to the mouth of the Scioto" (i.e., the area around Chillicothe, Ohio). Sadly, their home-built canoe sunk with all of their belongings, but the family managed to pull themselves ashore. They then set out on foot along the banks of the Scioto to the "mouth of the Paint" where they built a temporary camp. A year or so later they moved up to Highland County and lived on a "tributary of Fall creek [sic] called Grassy Branch."

As a result, I went to the Card Catalog and selected Maps, Atlases & Gazetteers > USA > 1800s > Ohio. I also used *Ohio* as a keyword. This filtering produced nine results. If I used Ohio in the Title search box, the only two returns were maps of an area I wasn't interested in. Because I didn't feel I could find a collection more specific to my search, I chose "U.S. Map Collection 1513–1990." As you can imagine, navigating this massive collection would be a challenge.

STEP ❷ Drill down deeper.

Next, once I clicked on the "U.S. Map Collection," I was given another search box; this time I added *Ohio* to the Map Title. One of the results was "Ohio County 1797–1803," which was at least in the right time period.

❶

- U.S., Indexed County Land Ownership Maps, 1860-1918
- U.S., Indexed Early Land Ownership and Township Plats, 1785-1898
- U.S. and World Atlases, 1822-1923
- U.S. Map Collection, 1513-1990
- Historic Land Ownership and Reference Atlases, 1507-2000
- Combination atlas map of Tuscarawas County, Ohio
- U.S. Gazetteer, 1854
- A complete genealogical, historical, chronological and geographical atlas
- Map and description of northeastern Ohio

❷

SEARCH   Match all terms exactly

	Year	Location
Any Event	——	City, County, State, Country
Publication Info		City, County, State, Country

Keyword

e.g. pilot or "Flying Tigers" ∨

Map Title

Ohio|

Topic

▾

SEARCH Clear search

STEP ❸ Review the map.

The resulting map (**A**) showed the Ohio and Scioto rivers meeting (as well as Chillicothe), but I would have to find another map to get into the detail of the Paint River, Fall Creek, and Grassy Branch.

As a side note, while searching for this map I found another (**B**) that beautifully illustrates why rivers were so widely chosen for travel. The rugged terrain throughout southern Pennsylvania and the area that is now West Virginia would have made overland passage to Ohio nearly impossible. Seeing this on a map helped me put my ancestors' journey in context—and made me appreciate the difficulty of early travel. For Americans of the period, rivers truly were the superhighways.

A

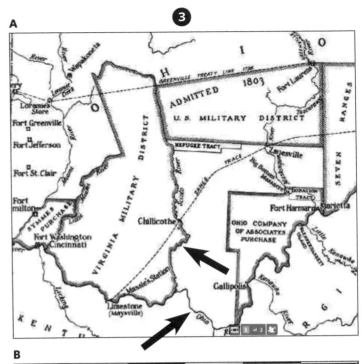

B

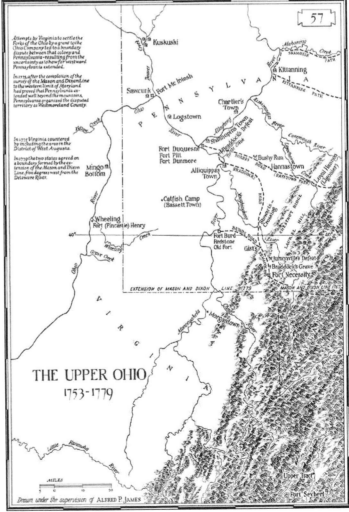

EXERCISE ③ Finding Historical Postcards

RESEARCH GOAL: *Find a postcard of Bruton Parish Church in Williamsburg, Virginia.*

STEP ❶ Search for collections.

Go to the Card Catalog and select the Pictures category, filtering for USA and adding *postcards* as a keyword. My results returned just one historical postcard collection. Note: If you only put *postcard* in the keyword box instead of *postcards*, you'll get zero results.

STEP ❷ Search for your locale.

I typed *Williamsburg Virginia* in the Location box and *bruton* in the Keyword(s) box. (The system automatically suggested Virginia when I typed *Williamsburg*.) As you can see, you also have the option of choosing the postcard "era." I used the pull-down arrow in the Postcard Era field to see available choices, which included items like Linen Era, Real Photo Era, and Divided Back Era.

❶

❷

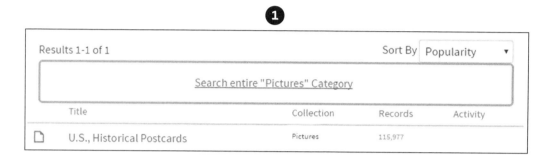

EXERCISE ③

STEP ❸ Narrow your search as necessary.

Because this search returned thousands of results, I had to add *bruton parish church* as a keyword and checked the Exact box (**A**). This forced the search engine to only return those specific results. Of the three results, one (**B**) was a lovely postcard from the Linen Era (circa 1930–1945).

A   ❸

SEARCH	Match all terms exactly

Location

Any Event   Williamsburg, Independent Cities, Virginia, USA

☐ Exact...

Keyword

bruton parish church   ☑ Exact

e.g. pilot or "Flying Tigers" ⌄

Postcard Era

▼

B

Bruton Parish Church,
Oldest Episcopal Church in Constant Use in America,
Williamsburg, Va.

EXERCISE ④   Finding an Obituary

RESEARCH GOAL: *Find an obituary for William Francis, who died in 2011 in Kansas City, Missouri.*

STEP ❶ Find your collection.

Go to the Card Catalog and choose the Newspapers & Publications category, then filter for Newspapers > USA > Missouri. This returned forty-one results. However, using keywords to limit my search didn't help, as adding *kansas city* produced zero results. I skimmed down the Location list and noticed that Jackson County (where Kansas City is located) wasn't listed as having any collection, so there was no point in trying to filter to a relevant Kansas City collection.

STEP ❷ Refine your search as necessary and review your results.

At this point, I felt the best course of action was to choose the large "U.S., Obituary Collection, 1930–2015" (**A**). Despite searching a much larger collection, I found the facts excerpted from the obituary (**B**).

In my experience, the large collection of Ancestry.com obituaries is particularly good when searching for fairly recent deaths. I have had little success, however, when searching for older obituaries.

❶

Filter By Location	
Audrain	4
Boone	3
Callaway	2
Cass	1
Cole	4
Jasper	2
Lafayette	1
Livingston	4
McDonald	1
Montgomery	1
Nodaway	1
Pettis	3
Randolph	3
Scott	1
St Clair	1

A   **❷**

| SEARCH | ☐ Match all terms exactly |

First & Middle Name(s)	Last Name
William	Francis
☐ Exact...	☐ Exact...

	Day	Month	Year	Location
Birth	▾	▾		City, County, St
Death	▾	▾	2011	City, County, St
			☐ Exact +/-...	

B

Name of Deceased:	William Francis
Gender:	Male
Age at Death:	75
Birth Date:	15 Oct 1935
Birth Place:	Eufaula, McIntosh, Oklahoma, USA
Residence (at time of death):	Kansas City, Missouri, USA
Death Date:	5 Mar 2011
Obituary Date:	12 Mar 2011
Spouse's Name:	Willa Francis
Parents' Names:	Thomas and Christie (Charty) Francis,
Childrens' Names:	Pam Francis and Lyn Francis

➤ Experiment with search terms by searching for a map by both state and county names in the Title or Keyword(s) box.

➤ Make liberal use of date filters; if your family didn't live in a specific place until 1870, filter for the 1800s.

➤ Leave the field for a person's name blank, then enter the place of interest in the Location box when searching for maps.

➤ Look for period maps of the colonies. For decades, rivers were the freeways of their time, as few roads existed outside the Atlantic coast. A period map that clearly shows major river systems might provide clues as to which river your family traveled on or along when migrating to a new place.

➤ Search picture collections based on what you're trying to accomplish. If you want a Civil War image, you'll need to filter down to the United States (location) and 1800s (or 1860s) as a time frame. Because your chances of finding a photo of your ancestor are slim (unless he was well-known or high-ranking), you may want to filter by keywords like state name, regiment, or type of unit (artillery, infantry, etc.).

➤ Concentrate on filtering by location and keyword if you're searching for historical photos of a place. Keep in mind, too, that many collections have search unique parameters; "U.S. Panoramic Photos, 1851–1991," for example, can be searched by location but not by a person's name. Oklahoma and Indian Territory photos can only be searched by keyword or caption.

➤ Search "U.S., School Yearbooks 1880–2012" if you're hoping to find a photo of your ancestor. It contains nearly 360 million images from around the country, making it your best bet for finding specific individuals; see chapter 7 for more on social history records. Second-best are the photos uploaded by Ancestry.com members, with images numbering more than 169 million.

➤ Remember that newspapers don't only contain obituaries. They can contain articles on bankruptcies, accidents, out-of-town visitors, neighborhood news, lists of missing person or people deemed insane, and police reports—in other words, anything and everything.

OBITUARY WORKSHEET AND EXTRACTION FORM

First, record key research details that will help you locate an ancestor's obituary.

Ancestor's name at death	
Other names used (including a maiden name)	
Known death and burial information	
Immediate family members	
Newspapers to check	

Once you find an obituary on Ancestry.com, extract the genealogical details about your ancestor.

Publication name			
Collection name			
Date accessed			
Deceased's name			
Date of death		**Place of death**	
Age at death		**Cause of death**	
Date of burial		**Place of burial**	
Date of birth		**Place of birth**	
Marital status		**Spouse's name**	
Surviving children's names			
Other surviving relatives' names			
Other deceased relatives' names			
Religious affiliation			
Community activities/hobbies			
Occupation/employment information			
Interesting biographical facts			
Funeral home or undertaker name/address			
Pallbearers			

NEWS-CLIPPING SOURCE WORKSHEET

Name	
Publication title, author, date, and page number	
Description of coverage	
Collection found/URL	
Notes	

Insert screenshot or paste printout of newspaper clippings featuring for ancestor here.

SOCIAL HISTORY

7

Social history is the study of the day-to-day lives of ordinary people. It searches for and analyzes the everyday experiences of our ancestors in the hopes of making sense of their lives and times. For example, future social historians will probably chronicle our age with stories about our media consumption, bevy of gadgets, cultural pursuits, and political processes. And genealogists can make these kinds of observations by studying the life and times of our ancestors.

As no collections on Ancestry.com are labeled "social history," where do you find those fascinating facts that turn a compilation of names and dates into a living, breathing person? Ancestry.com has a number of collections categories that cover social history:

- Schools, Directories & Church Histories
- Stories, Memories & Histories
- Wills, Probates, Land, Tax & Criminal
- Family Trees

These four categories represent million of records and endless opportunities for discovering your ancestors' social history. To make it a little easier, I'll give you an overview of each broad group of collections and tips for effectively searching them.

SCHOOLS, DIRECTORIES & CHURCH HISTORIES

This is the collection that contains information on home, church, school, and business life, giving you an overview of what your ancestor's daily life might have been like.

City & Area Directories and Telephone Directories

City directories can contain surprisingly useful, detailed information. In addition to the head of household's name, they can also list the names of other people living in the home, their martial status (e.g., "married" or "widow"), occupation, and even death dates (image **A**). Ancestry.com's city directories date from 1822 and continue through 1995.

If you can't find your family in one city directory, try searching the same directory and choosing a different year. It's possible your ancestor didn't live in that particular city until after the year's directory was compiled.

"Telephone Directories" are a slightly different breed of animal from a city directory; the "U.S. Phone and Address Directories" covers 1993 through 2002, while the "U.S. Public Records Index" covers 1950 through 1993. In both of these, you can find names and addresses, plus occupations and birth dates.

A

> ROOSEVELT FRANKLIN D (Anna Eleanor), Governor State of New York, President-Elect of the United States of America, N Y Residence 49 E 65th
> " Franklin D Mrs (Val-Kill Shop) h49 E 65th
> " Fredk Mrs h330 Park av apt 9 B
> " Fur Dressing Co Inc (NY) 159 W 27th
> " Furniture Co Inc (cap $40,000) Saml Bonnet pres-sec Ma Harrison treas 2341 8th av

City directories list your ancestor's name, address, housemates, marital status, occupation, and sometimes death dates.

School Lists & Yearbooks

The largest collection in this broad collection is that of "U.S. School Yearbooks. 1880–2012," briefly mentioned in chapter 6. This whopper collection covers yearbooks for students in middle school, junior high school, high school, and colleges across the United States.

If you're lucky enough to know the name of the yearbook, add it to your search form, as this will help narrow down search results—especially if your ancestor lived in a city where there were numerous schools.

Church Histories & Records

These are the collections to search if you hope to find your ancestor listed as a church member in a specific church or if you have Quaker ancestors. This collection contains Hinshaw's famous "Index to Quaker Meeting Records," as well as many other collections of Quaker records.

Because there are close to two thousand collections in this subcategory, remember to make extensive use of location, date, and keyword filters.

If you're searching for non-US records, this subcategory is still of interest to you, as it includes 150 collections and millions of European church records. You can find parish records, birth and baptismal records, and marriage records and banns.

In my experience, this is one of those instances in which there are so many potential collections that if your initial "filtered" search is unsuccessful, you should search the entire subcategory by clicking on the link located at the top of the list (image **B**).

Professional & Organizational Directories

This is almost a free-for-all resource, as it spans records as diverse as railroad employee records, state hospital records, Red Cross nurse files, and lists of Masonic Society members. If you're searching for a US ancestor, be sure to pick USA as a location filter, or you'll have to wade through over two hundred European collections.

Once you use the USA filter, you'll still have access to more than 750 collections, so filter further either by state, date, or keyword.

STORIES, MEMORIES & HISTORIES

This is probably in my top three list of favorite Ancestry.com resources. Who doesn't love old stories? There are six separate collections here, and they are simply loaded with family, social, and place histories. In addition, you'll find the "Biography & Genealogy Master Index (BGMI)" that can point you to published genealogies and biographies that are not digitized.

B

Results 1-25 of 2,132		Sort By	Popularity ▼

Search entire "Church Histories & Records" Category

Title	Collection	Records	Activity
Sweden, Church Records, 1451-1943 (in Swedish)	Church Histories & Records	35,250,410	UPDATED
Pennsylvania and New Jersey, Church and Town Records, 1708-1985	Church Histories & Records	10,934,013	
U.S., Quaker Meeting Records, 1681-1935	Church Histories & Records	6,427,235	
West Yorkshire, England, Church of England Marriages and Banns, 1813-1935	Church Histories & Records	2,525,369	

Search the entire Church Histories & Records subcategory if your filtered search doesn't return the appropriate results.

Using the Title field—rather than the Keyword(s)—can lead to different results, such as this Title search for *Maryland*.

Family Histories, Journals & Biographies

With more than seventeen thousand collections in this subcategory, you'll have to make good use of filters. If you're hoping to find a history of one of your ancestral families, filter not only by location but also by keyword. If you're among the lucky, you'll type your last name in as a keyword and see a lovely family biography. But the rest of us will have to rely more on location filters such as state and county.

For example, I couldn't find a mention of my family by filtering for Missouri > Jackson County. But once in the collection "A Memorial and biographical record of Kansas City and Jackson County, Mo.," I was able to read more about Lone Jack, the little town in which they lived.

Oral Histories & Interviews

With only twenty collections, this subcategory of transcripts won't serve much purpose to you unless you happen to be looking for pioneer ancestors in Oklahoma and Indian Territory, Ellis Island oral histories, or slave narratives.

Social & Place Histories

Here you'll find those juicy county histories that chronicle the early settlers of the county, including their origins (e.g., Wales), possibly their military background, the names of their spouses and children, their professions, and where they lived. Again, this is a huge subcategory with more than twenty thousand collections.

If your family settled a colony or a county in the early days, filter either by state and/or state and county. If Europe is your target, you'll find a healthy selection of collections, particularly in the United Kingdom (more than seven hundred) and Germany (more than eight hundred). Even tiny Liechtenstein has nine collections listed.

Something important to remember: Perhaps you want to find some mention of a Maryland ancestor who settled around Baltimore in the early 1700s. If you filter the Card Catalog with USA > Maryland, the Ancestry.com system will return all collections that include Maryland but are not *exclusively* Maryland. In this instance, I suggest typing *Maryland* in the Title box; this forces the system to return only those collections that have the word *Maryland* in the title. But even setting up those search parameters, you'll still get 120 collections (image **C**), so filter by keyword and county as well.

Society & Organization Histories

This subcategory is another hodgepodge of collections, from lineage society records to statistics on baseball players to records of Revolutionary War-era Loyalists. Before even beginning to filter, you should skim through the first three or four pages of collections just to get a sense of the types of collections in this subcategory.

Once you narrow down your goal, start filtering by location. For example, if you're interested in joining a lineage society, use *lineages* in the Title or Keyword(s) box. If your search is for Revolutionary War-era information, be sure to use the 1700s date filter.

Military Histories

As you would expect, these six-hundred-plus collections include rosters, regimental histories, and state-specific military histories (e.g., "The Union Regiments of Kentucky"). Filter by date and location to locate the collections that best match where you think your ancestor can be found.

If you're interested in the Civil War history of any regiment, don't miss "Official records of the Union and Confederate Armies, 1861–1865." This colossal work is a compilation of official records of both Union and Confederate Armies, with references to orders, operations, and formal reports. You can search this collection by name, date, location, or keyword. If you use the keyword search to look for a regiment name, be sure to put the name of the regiment in quotation marks so Ancestry will search for that exact phrase (e.g., *18th Missouri*").

See chapter 4 for more on military-related records.

Royalty, Nobility & Heraldry

This is a subcategory for everyone who hopes to find they're descended from royalty. As you can imagine, there are only a handful of US collections, with the remaining 120-plus relevant to Europe.

WILLS, PROBATES, LAND, TAX & CRIMINAL

The records in this category lean more toward legal issues. They range from land-ownership issues to court, bank, and insurance records, plus documents dealing with wills and disposition of property.

Land Records

Land records are valuable because they place an ancestor in a specific location during a specific period of time. They can also describe family relationships and—in the case of bounty land warrants—military service. The Land Records Worksheet at the end of the chapter can help you keep track of these resources.

Tax Lists

The taxman has been around in some form or another about as long as America has. Taxation

records may include indexes and images of tax records taken by a state or county auditor. You'll also find "U.S., IRS Tax Assessment Lists, 1862–1918," a collection of documents related to filing tax reports to the Internal Revenue Service and its predecessor, the Bureau of Internal Revenue. In addition to tax lists for land you can also find valuations for things like numbers of livestock.

The Tax Records Worksheet at the end of the chapter can help you keep track of these resources.

Court, Governmental & Criminal Records

Records here relate to criminal cases, prison rolls, and divorce cases—in other words, just about any kind of issue that went through a formal legal process. If your ancestors were Native American, you may find them in the collection "U.S., Native American Applications for Enrollment in the Five Civilized Tribes, 1898–1914."

You might be surprised at all you can learn in a criminal record. In the collection "Texas, Convict and Conduct Registers, 1875–1945," for example, you'll find all of the standard descriptors like height, weight, and eye color, plus the person's use of tobacco, identifying marks (e.g., "crooked little finger right hand"), date and place of birth, date and length of incarceration, and offense.

Wills & Probates, Estates & Guardian Records

Wills and probate records can often be a jackpot for genealogists. These are the records that name family members, relationships, witnesses, and any possessions. You can find some full records, while others are indexes and still more are abstracts (in which salient information has been extracted from a will or probate). If you're not sure where to start, you might have better luck by searching all of the Wills & Probates, Estates & Guardian Records subcategory instead of starting in individual collections. (See Exercise #4.)

See the Estate Records Worksheet and the US Probate Records Checklist at the end of this chapter for help keeping track of these resources.

Bank & Insurance Records

These sound boring, don't they? But be sure to search them anyway! This subcategory has a number of gems waiting to be found. Here, you'll find "Freedman's

D

No. 487 RECORD for *William Young*

Date, *April 24 1871*
Where born, *In the South*
Where brought up,
Residence, *118 Upper St*
Age, *10* Complexion, *Dark Brown*
Occupation, *Errand boy in Grocery*
Works for *Archie Young his father*
Wife or Husband,
Children,

Father, *Archie Young*
Mother, *Irene " "*
Brothers and Sisters, *Austin Lippie*

Bank records, such as this one from the Freedman's Bank, provides clues for researching more distant ancestors—in this case, the names of the slave ancestor's owner and parents.

Bank Records, 1865–1871," an index to the Freedman's Savings and Trust Company's registers, particularly useful if you have African-American ancestors who were freed slaves. Some of the records include the name of the slave-born ancestor's former master or mistress, a piece of information that can take you back a generation or so in your research (image **D**). This subcategory also contains the "New York Emigrant

Savings Bank, 1850–1883," records from a bank established specifically for Irish immigrants.

FAMILY TREES

Although not created specifically as a social history tool, a search for public family trees can reveal information relating to social history (image **E**), such as:

- photographs
- document scans
- newspaper scans
- family stories and legends
- biographies

Photographs offer a glimpse into the fashion of the day. If you're not sure of the time period the photo was taken, spend some time reading Maureen Taylor's *Photo Detective* blog. **<blog.familytreemagazine.com/photodetectiveblog>**. There, you'll find great tips on placing photos within a specific time frame.

I also like using newspaper scans found in family trees, not only for obituaries but for any article relating to the family. This could be about visiting relatives, a significant event, an accident, or an injury.

If you're lucky, another researcher might also have added an ancestral biography to the tree. These are sometimes filled with family legends (not sourced), and other times they provide wonderful stories that you'll never find anywhere else.

E

All Public Member Trees results for Smith

Search Filters	Broad — Exact

Smith
BORN: Cincinnati

Edit Search | New Search | UPDATE

Family Trees

Public Member Trees

This database contains family trees submitted to Ancestry by users who have indicated that their tree can be viewed by all Ancestry subscribers. These trees can change over time as users edit,...

Results 1–50 of 193

Member Tree	Name	Parents
	Loris D Smith 1	
rita,s tree-1	Birth: 21 Sep 1912 - Appanoose, USA	F: George Milton Smith 1
Public Member Tree 7 attached records, 8 sources 📷 photos	Death: 12 Jan 2001 - Saint Petersburg, Pinellas, Florida, United States of America Marriage: 9 Jun 1946 - Unionville, Putnam, Missouri, United States Spouse: John Harold Findlay 1	M: Luella Sarah James 1
rita s tree-1_SyncBackup_634859890147308805	Loris D Smith 1	F: George Milton Smith 1
Public Member Tree 4 attached records, 5 sources	Birth: 21 Sep 1912 - Appanoose, USA Death: 12 Jan 2001 - Clearwater, Pinellas, Florida, USA	M: Luella Sarah James 1

Data uploaded by other Ancestry.com members, such as photographs and family stories, are often searchable and can be potential sources of information.

RESEARCH GOAL: *See if anyone with the surname Heitkemper lived in Portland, Oregon, in the nineteenth century (and, if they did, find what their address was).*

STEP ❶ Find your collection.

Since there's not a single "Social History" subcategory, go instead to the Card Catalog and filter for Schools, Directories & Church Histories, then City & Area Directories. I filtered by Location: USA > Oregon > Multnomah County, resulting in only one result: "Portland, Oregon Directories, 1890–91."

STEP ❷ Fill out last name box, then leave everything else blank.

Why not fill out more boxes, you ask? I knew the Heitkemper I was looking for was a jeweler, but I didn't know for sure if the business dealt just with jewelry or it worked with other trades as well, and I didn't know the location. My guess was that there weren't that many people with that last name living in Portland in that time period.

❶

	Title	Collection	Records	Activity
📄	Portland, Oregon Directories, 1890-91	City & Area Directories	62,119	

Results 1-1 of 1   Sort By Popularity ▾

Search entire "City & Area Directories" Category

❷

SEARCH   ☐ Match all terms exactly

First & Middle Name(s)

Last Name
heitkemper

☐ Exact…

	Year	Location
Lived In	—	City, County, State, Country
Any Event		City, County, State, Country

Keyword

e.g. pilot or "Flying Tigers" ⌄

Business Name

Occupation

☐ Exact

Location 1

STEP ❸ Analyze your search results.

Of the sixteen Heitkempers listed, Gerhard was listed as being involved with clocks, watches, jewelry, and diamonds; Gerhard Jr. and Frank were both listed as watchmakers. I knew this was the right family.

What next? Between the three Gerhards, I had four addresses: 55 Morrison corner 3d, 46 Grant, 151 3d, and 405 8th. I could stop and say "Mission accomplished" at this point, but I wanted to see if these addresses still exist. That would involve leaving Ancestry.com and going to Google Maps **<www.google.com/maps>** or Google Earth **<www.google.com/earth>**. But before I could even do that, I would need to find where these addresses would fit into present-day Portland, as the city streets are now all named with prefixes of NE, SE, NW, or NE—a research project for another day.

Results 1–10 of 16

View Record	Name	Location 1	Location 2	Occupation
	To get better results, add more information such as **First Name, Birth Info, Death Info or Location**—even a guess will help. Edit your search or learn more.			
View Record	Anna M Heitkemper		boards 89 3d.	clk
View Record	Francis M Heitkemper		boards 229 Chapman.	clk
View Record	Frank A Heitkemper		boards 405 8th.	clk
View Record	Gerhard Heitkemper; Watches Diamonds	151 3d	405 8th.	Clocks and Jewelry
View Record	Gerhard Heitkemper, Jr		boards 405 8th.	clk
View Record	Henry Heitkemper	130 3d	89 3d.	Mngr Wines and Liquors
View Record	Herman Heitkemper	63 Williams	same.	cigar mnfr
View Record	John G Heitkemper		boards 63 Williams.	student
View Record	Mary L Heitkemper		boards 89 3d.	clk
View Record	Frank A Heitkemper		boards 46 Grant.	watchmkr

1–10 of 16   Per page 10 ▼   1   2   ▶

EXERCISE ②   Finding an Ancestor in a Yearbook

RESEARCH GOAL: *Find my aunt Helen Hendrickson in a yearbook.*

STEP ❶ Find a collection to search.
Go to the Card Catalog and filter for Schools, Directories & Church Histories, then filter by Collection (School List and Yearbooks) and by Location (USA > Missouri). Of the eleven available collections, I selected "U.S., School Yearbooks, 1880–2012."

STEP ❷ Enter your search terms.
Search by name (*Helen Hendrickson*) and location (**A**). Within the results were four listings for "my" Helen Hendrickson (**B**).

STEP ❸ Review your results.
I found treasure! Images of my aunt when she was in her teens—and interestingly how much my sister looks like her!

1

Results 1-11 of 11		Sort By	Popularity ▼

Search entire "School Lists & Yearbooks" Category

Title	Collection	Records	Activity
📄 U.S., School Yearbooks, 1880-2012	School Lists & Yearbooks	359,973,906	
📄 U.S., School Catalogs, 1765-1935	School Lists & Yearbooks	5,378,762	
📄 U.S., World War II Cadet Nursing Corps Card Files, 1942-1948	School Lists & Yearbooks	390,020	
📄 U.S., College Student Lists, 1763-1924	School Lists & Yearbooks	1,516,361	
📄 U.S., High School Student Lists, 1821-1923	School Lists & Yearbooks	645,940	

A

SEARCH ☐ Match all terms exactly

First & Middle Name(s)	Last Name
Helen	Hendrickson
☐ Exact...	☐ Exact...

	Year	Location
Birth		——
Lived In	——	Saint Joseph, Buchanan, Missouri, USA
		☐ Exact...
Any Event		City, County, State, Country

B

View Record	Name	School	School Location	Year	Yearbook Title	View Image
View Record	Helen Hendrickson	Central High School	St Joseph, Missouri, USA	1938	The Wakitan	
View Record	Helen Hendrickson	Central High School	St. Joseph, Missouri, USA	1936		
View Record	Helen Hendrickson	Central High School	St Joseph, Missouri	1937	Wakitan 1937	
View Record	Helen Hendrickson	Central High School	St. Joseph, Missouri, USA	1937		

3

EXERCISE ③ Finding and Using a County History

RESEARCH GOAL: *Locate a history of Tippecanoe County, Indiana.*

STEP ❶ Find your collection.

Go to the Card Catalog and filter for Stories, Memories & Histories, then Social & Place Histories. I also filtered by Location: USA > Indiana. This filtering still left more than seven thousand possible collections! Far too many to search.

STEP ❷ Limit your search by county.

Under the list of Indiana counties, you can see there are two collections relative to Tippecanoe County (**A**). Click on Tippecanoe to add it to your filters (**B**).

STEP ❸ Review your results.

Because the results show only two collections, I will search both of them, hoping to find some mention of last name *Dimmitt*. Guess what? Both volumes mentioned the family, including the fact that they lived in Tennessee before coming to Indiana—another clue to follow as I had no idea the Dimmitts were ever in Tennessee. As you can see, this opens up a whole new avenue of research.

Note: If your family settled in a county early in its formation, it's possible you'll find them mentioned by name in biographies, political discussions, names of storekeepers, pioneer houses, court records, and even information about the family's origin. These books are among my very favorite for finding those wonderful details about the family.

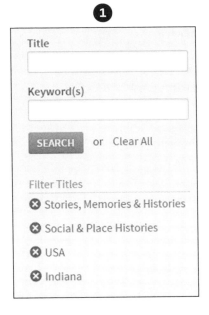

A

Switzerland	18
Tippecanoe	2
Tipton	1
Union	1

B

Filter Titles
- ❌ Stories, Memories & Histories
- ❌ Social & Place Histories
- ❌ USA
- ❌ Indiana
- ❌ Tippecanoe

Results 1-2 of 2   Sort By [Popularity ▾]

Search entire "Social & Place Histories" Category

Title	Collection	Records	Activity
📄 Biographical record and portrait album of Tippecanoe County, Indiana : containing portraits of all the presidents of the United	Social & Place Histories	791	
📄 Past and present of Tippecanoe County, Indiana	Social & Place Histories	1,350	

EXERCISE ④ Finding and Analyzing a Will

RESEARCH GOAL: *Find legal records for some of my Faulkenberry ancestors.*

STEP ❶ Find your collection.

Go to the Card Catalog and filter for Wills, Probate, Land, Tax & Criminal, then USA > Wills & Probates, Estates & Guardian Records. This resulted in 316 collections. Because I had no idea which member of the family to search for, I clicked the link to "Search entire Wills & Probates, Estates & Guardian Records Category" and used only two search parameters: last name and death location. I specified that death location (Missouri) was exact, as many people in Georgia and South Carolina had that last name in the search results.

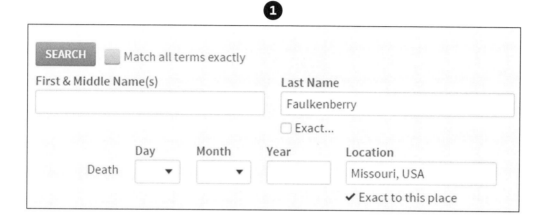

STEP ❷ Review your results.

This search resulted in eleven entries, among them my great-grandfather, Frank Faulkenberry (**A**). The available information was not a will, but rather an "administrator's bond" (**B**). Administrators are usually required to post a bond with the court, with two or more sureties (someone who agrees to be liable for someone else's debt or performance), until the estate is settled. In this instance, my great-grandmother was the administrator and her three daughters were sureties.

 The administrator is promising that she will faithfully perform the duties required of her. Based on this (and the fact that her daughters were sureties), everyone would have been confident the family will make good on debts should they arise before the estate is settled.

A

Missouri, Wills and Probate Records, 1766-1988
WILLS & PROBATES, ESTATES & GUARDIAN RECORDS

View Image

NAME: Frank **Faulkenberry**
DEATH: Abt 1911 - Missouri, USA

B

②

Know all Men by these Presents, That I, Sarah G Fauldenberry as Principal,
and we, *Rosa Bell Fauldenberry, Edith May Helmig & Bessie Francis Fauldenberry*
as Sureties, are held and firmly bound unto the State of Missouri, in the full and just sum of
Two Thousand (2000) **Dollars,**
to the payment whereof well and truly to be made, we bind ourselves, our heirs, executors, administrators and assigns, jointly and severally.
firmly by these presents.
Sealed with our seals and dated at *Lone Creek* Mo., this *21st* day of *October*, A. D. *1902*
THE CONDITION OF THE ABOVE BOND IS, That if *Sarah G Fauldenberry*

Administrat*rix* of the Estate of *Frank C Fauldenberry* deceased, shall faithfully administer said
Estate, account for, pay and deliver all money and property of said Estate, and perform all other things touching said administration required by
law or the order or decree of any Court having jurisdiction, then the above Bond to be void, otherwise to remain in full force.

Bessie Francis Fauldenberry   *Sarah G Fauldenberry*
Bond approved   *Rosa Bell Fauldenberry*
J E Guinotte Judge   *Edith May Helmig*

I certify that the above bond was signed and executed in my presence the day and date above written.

(Dist) *Term Expires Dec 21 1911*   *J C Jackson Notary Public*

What might this tell you? Perhaps a few things:

1. The family had enough cash or access to cash to settle debts.
2. The deceased didn't have enough debt for the family to worry about.
3. The deceased owned enough property that it could serve as collateral against debts.

STEP ❸ Search for other records to learn more.

Next, I would search for land records to learn how much land the deceased might have owned. Then, I would search for marriage records for the three daughters; it's possible they were all married by this time and thus had the ability to settle debts.

❸

U.S. General Land Office Records, 1796-1907

[SEARCH] ☐ Match all terms exactly

First & Middle Name(s)   Last Name

Day   Month   Year   Location
Any Event   ▼   ▼   City, County, State, Count

Keyword

e.g. pilot or "Flying Tigers" ▾

Acres

Land Office

Browse this collection

To browse this image set, select from the options below.

State
Choose... ▼

County

Related data collections

U.S., Indexed County Land Ownership Maps, 1860-1918
This database contains approximately 1,200 U.S. county land ownership atlases from the Library of Congress' Geography and Maps division, covering the approximate years 1864-1918. Some

 Missouri, Wills and Probate Records, 1766-1988

(89 total images in packet)

WILLS & PROBATES, ESTATES & GUARDIAN RECORDS

View Image

NAME: J D **Faulkenberry**

DEATH: **Missouri, USA**

RESEARCH GOAL: *Dig deeper into the Faulkenberry family affairs and put together a more thorough picture of my ancestors' lives.*

STEP ❶ Identify a starting point.

Remember the eleven results from the last search? One of them was Frank's brother Jacob David (J.D.). Note that the results tell me there are eighty-nine total images in this probate package, so I'm positive there's much to be learned here.

STEP ❷ Open the inventory and review the table of contents.

J.D.'s probate file includes inventories, sales, and accounts of his estate. Using this information makes it easier to flesh out the details of how he lived—and hopefully offer some insight into the life of my own great-grandfather.

Name:	J D Faulkenberry
Probate Place:	Jackson, Missouri, USA
Inferred Death Place:	Missouri, USA
Item Description:	Case Files, Series 2, Box 42, Files 6-25, Euneau-Fields

Table of Contents	89 images
Cover Page	1
Petition Papers	2
Administration Papers	3–4
Petition Papers	5
Inventory Papers	6–21
Order Papers	22–32
Account Papers	33–41
Sales Paper	42–43
Account Papers	44–47
Sales Paper	48–56
Account Papers	57–68
Sales Paper	69–73
Account Papers	74–75
Petition Papers	76–80
Account Papers	81–89

STEP ❸ Read the file and draw conclusions.

Among my findings: J.D. owned several acres of land and (more interestingly) 1,150 shares of a gold-mining operation in Arizona. Now how did he get into that? Another mystery for another day.

The inventory details an assortment of his belongings: six tons of hay, a black stallion, a brown mare, thirty-three gallons of lard, twelve chairs, a sewing machine, twenty-nine gallons of canned fruit, three Jersey steers, and sixty-three yards of carpet. An inventory not only catalogues property, but also value. This information goes a long way towards building a solid understanding of a person's everyday life. Based on this, I would say J.D. did quite well for his time, and my next task will be finding an obituary for him.

❸

➤ Think more about "time" and "place" and less about last name when using Social History to fill in details about an ancestor's life. You may never find your ancestor listed in a book, but you can find information about where he lived.

➤ Use the US census as the backbone of your research. In every federal census from 1850 onwards, you'll find your ancestor's occupation listed. Once you know the decade and occupation, search digitized books and histories for mention of that trade or industry. The 1850 and 1870 censuses show the value of real property (land) owned by each person, so you can compare your ancestor's holdings to those around him. The 1900 to 1940 censuses will also tell you whether your ancestor owned or rented his home, and the 1910 and 1920 censuses will even tell if home or farm "owners" owned their property free and clear or had a mortgage.

➤ Check the agricultural census schedules for 1850 to 1880 if your ancestor was a farmer. You'll find these in the Ancestry.com collection "Selected U.S. Federal Census Non-Population Schedules, 1850–1880."

➤ Add the name of your ancestor's religious denomination in the Keyword(s) box in the Card Catalog to learn more about the type of church your ancestor attended, even if you haven't found your ancestor in a published church history. For example, one Methodist collection that can tell you about how your ancestors may have practiced their religion is "A history of Methodism in Alabama."

➤ Keep location in mind. Some church records, for example, are listed by county and not denomination.

CITY DIRECTORIES WORKSHEET

Use this form to organize information that can aid your search for ancestors in city directories on Ancestry.com. If you're not sure of a detail, leave it blank or provide your best guess(es) based on research you've done. Update the information as you uncover new records.

Ancestor information

Original name: _____ Life dates: _____

Cities of residence (years of residence and address, if known): _____

_____

Year	Name	Address	Collection

LAND RECORDS WORKSHEET

Use this form to organize information that can aid your search for ancestors' land patents and deeds on Ancestry.com. If you're not sure of a detail, leave it blank or provide your best guess(es) based on research you've done. Update the information as you uncover new records.

Ancestor information

Original name: _____

Spelling variants/other names used: _____

Birth date: _____ Birthplace: _____

Ancestor's known places of residence

Place	Address	Dates of residence

Land records searched

Collection name	Search terms used	Date searched

TAX RECORDS WORKSHEET

Use this form to organize information that can aid your search for ancestors' tax records on Ancestry.com. If you're not sure of a detail, leave it blank or provide your best guess(es) based on research you've done. Update the information as you uncover new records.

Ancestor information

Original name: _____

Birth date: _____   Birthplace: _____

Residences during lifetime

State/territory	County/parish	Town/township	Dates

Federal tax checklist

Check each box below if an ancestor was of taxable age during the years indicated; include any checked years in the chronology below.

☐ 1798 Direct

☐ 1813, 1815 Direct

☐ 1861 Direct

☐ 1862–1872 Income

Tax list extraction form

List your ancestor chronologically as he/she appeared in tax records (as available). Different types of taxes will yield different information: Sometimes the record that has survived will vary from year to year, either due to record-keeping practices or changes in the actual law.

Year	Name (as spelled on list)	Type (poll, property, etc.)	Notes (tax amounts, acres, personal property)

ESTATE RECORDS WORKSHEET

Use this form to organize information you find in wills, probate files and other records of a deceased ancestor's estate on Ancestry.com. Add to this form as you discover more information.

Ancestor's name	
Death date	
County of death/burial	
Estate record found? **If so, list when and where**	
Were the estate proceedings testate **(deceased left a will)** **or intestate (no will)?**	☐ testate ☐ intestate ☐ unknown
Date of will	
Date of petition to initiate probate	
Date of final settlement	

People named	In which document?	Notes (role in estate, relationship to deceased, major bequests received)

What else do estate documents reveal about this ancestor?	
Avenues for further research estate documents suggest (look for deeds, etc)	
Others' estates that may mention this ancestor as an heir	

US LEGAL RECORDS CHECKLIST

Ancestor's name	
Residence/location (include town/city, county, and state names)	
Dates lived in that location	
Spouse's name	
Children's names	

Types of records to look for

Put a checkmark next to each record type after you've searched available records on Ancestry.com for the ancestor listed above. Cross off any record types that aren't available on Ancestry.com for your ancestor's residence location and time period.

Record type	Date searched
☐ Bonds	
☐ Civil court case records	
☐ Criminal court case records	
☐ Estate files/records	
☐ Estate inventories	
☐ Freedman's Bank records	
☐ Freedmen's Bureau Field Office records	
☐ Guardianship records	
☐ Land records (deeds, grants, patents, tract books)	
☐ Naturalizations	
☐ Orphan records	
☐ Probate files	
☐ Tax lists/records	
☐ Vital records (births, marriages, deaths, divorces)	
☐ Voter lists/records	
☐ Wills/will books	
☐ Other _____	

Adapted from *Unofficial Guide to FamilySearch.org*. Copyright © 2015 Dana McCullough

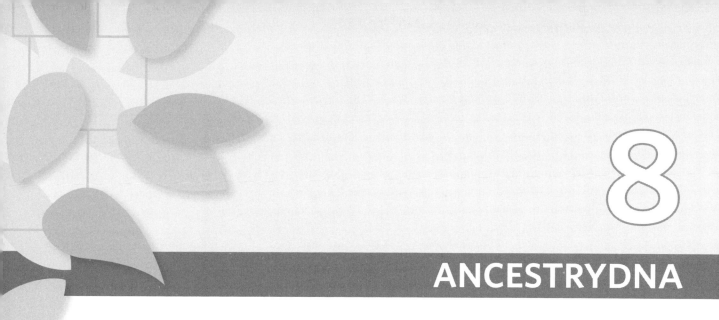

8

ANCESTRYDNA

Genetic genealogy—research that uses DNA to connect family lines—has grown in popularity not only in the genealogy world but also across disciplines, most notably archaeology and medicine. In recent times, DNA findings have confirmed that humans still carry a small percentage of Neanderthal DNA, while remains of early Irish farmers contain DNA that originated near the Mediterranean. DNA analysis has even found DNA fragments of olives and oregano in ceramic jars from an ancient Greek ship-wreck. It seems that DNA news is everywhere.

In some cases, DNA has unlocked long-unknown family lines; in others, it has shattered lines once held as true. The latter is evidenced in news like the discovery that the Archbishop of Canterbury's DNA suggests a surprising paternal parentage. But whether it opens new lines of research or shuts down others, DNA is being used more and more to help genealogists discover their true origins.

While Ancestry.com wasn't the first genealogy-based company to delve into DNA, it has rapidly become the best-known and most popular. By mid-2015, it had tested more than one million people and delivered ninety-nine million connections of fourth cousins or closer; by mid-2016, the number of tested individuals had doubled to two million.

Here's how DNA testing from Ancestry.com works:

1. Order your test kit ($99) at **<dna.ancestry.com>**; your kit will arrive with a container and a pre-paid return envelope.

2. Follow the kit's instructions by taking a saliva sample, putting it in the container provided, and mailing the sealed kit back to Ancestry.com.

3. In six to eight weeks, you'll receive an e-mail link to your results. From there, you'll interpret results—which is what we'll be discussing in this chapter.

What can you do once you receive your results? Let's find out.

REVIEWING YOUR TEST RESULTS

Once your test results are online, you'll have plenty of information to get started in your ancestry search. The results estimate your ethnic makeup across twenty-six geographical regions. It also identifies potential relatives based on matches to other people who have taken the test. In this section, I'll walk you through the various sections on your DNA home page and talk about how best to use each section to further your research.

Log on to your Ancestry.com account and click DNA in the top menu.

Your DNA home page consists of three sections:

1. Your ethnicity estimates and a thumbnail of DNA matches (image **A**)
2. New Ancestor Discoveries (image **B**)
3. DNA Circles (image **C**)

Ethnicity Estimates

Click See Full Ethnicity Estimate from your DNA home page to see both a chart (image **D**) and a map

A

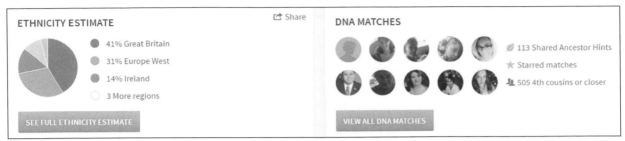

From your DNA home page (once you've taken an AncestryDNA test and have received your results), you can view your ethnicity estimate and a summary of your DNA matches.

B

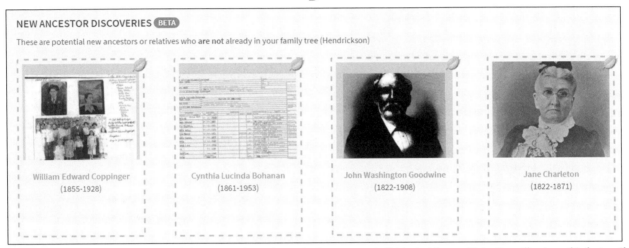

The New Ancestor Discoveries feature links your results to those of other users and of historical figures. Note: You will not see this feature if your results haven't matched with any New Ancestry Discoveries.

C

DNA Circles represent groups of users who share DNA (or likely share DNA) with each other.

(image **E**) of your genetic estimates. These calculations estimate the percentage of your DNA that shares segments with people native to a particular country or region, approximating where the ancestors who gave you your DNA came from. See the quick guide to ethnicity estimate global regions at the end of this chapter to learn more about these regions and subregions.

Discovering your ethnicity is exciting and, at times, puzzling. You may know that you're basically of European origin, but your European origins may turn out to include Ireland, Scandinavia, Western Europe, and Great Britain. In my case, I had 14-percent Irish heritage, a surprising estimate as I've only found one distant ancestor from Ireland so far. As you can imagine, finding that Irish ethnicity is both a puzzle and a research challenge.

Keep in mind that these ethnicity calculations are only estimates. As you'll notice by clicking on each ethnicity in the chart, your actual percentage of DNA shared from a particular region will vary greatly. In addition, you don't have DNA from all of your direct-line ancestors, meaning not all your ancestors' birthplaces will necessarily be included in your ethnicity estimate. As a result, don't take your ethnicity estimate as final or absolute.

By clicking a region's name, you can also access another valuable research tool in this section of your DNA page, as each will contain information about the region and its inhabitants. For example, when I click on Scandinavia, a new page of information is launched. Here I can read about the genetic diversity of the area, a brief history of the region, and immigration and migration patterns of people from this region. It also shows how I genetically compare to people who are native to Scandinavia.

For even more information, click Help, located at the top of every ethnicity page. A box will pop up with even more information to help you understand your DNA results (image **F**). For example, you can learn how trace regions are determined or why you may have more or less of a certain region than is estimated.

DNA Matches

At the top of your DNA home page, click View All DNA Matches. The next page shows all of the people who match your DNA, organized (by default) by date or relationship (for example, Close Family, First Cousin, Second Cousin, etc.). At the top of this page

D

REGION	APPROXIMATE AMOUNT
Europe	100%
■ Great Britain	41%
■ Europe West	31%
■ Ireland	14%
▢ Scandinavia	10%
⊖ Trace Regions ❓	4%
▢ Iberian Peninsula	3%
■ Italy/Greece	1%

Your ethnicity estimate is given as an approximate percentage across various geographic regions.

E

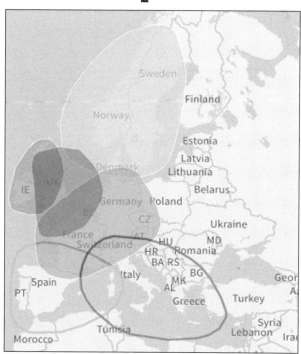

Your ethnicity estimate is also displayed visually over a map of the associated region (in my case, Europe).

are three filters you can use to organize results (image **G**), though Relationship order is the default setting.

This is the section that can be the most valuable and the most frustrating: valuable because you're finding people who match your DNA—sometimes as close as a first or second cousin—and frustrating because many of them have not uploaded or con-

F

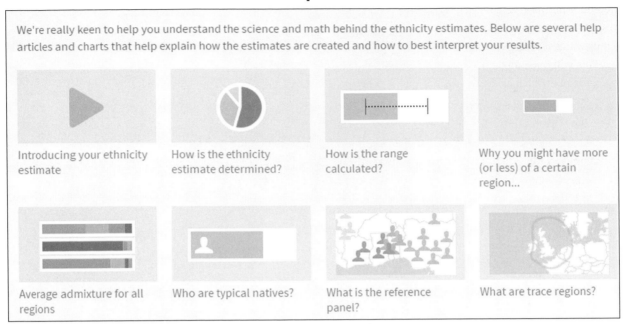

We're really keen to help you understand the science and math behind the ethnicity estimates. Below are several help articles and charts that help explain how the estimates are created and how to best interpret your results.

Introducing your ethnicity estimate

How is the ethnicity estimate determined?

How is the range calculated?

Why you might have more (or less) of a certain region...

Average admixture for all regions

Who are typical natives?

What is the reference panel?

What are trace regions?

AncestryDNA's Help section walks you through various aspects of your DNA results.

G

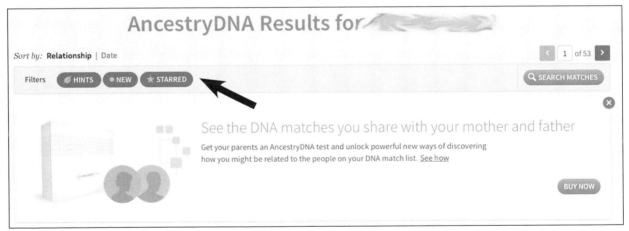

You can use three filters when viewing your DNA matches: Hints (i.e., whether Ancestry.com has identified a Hint for shared matches), New (i.e., matches you haven't reviewed), and Starred (i.e., matches you have flagged).

H

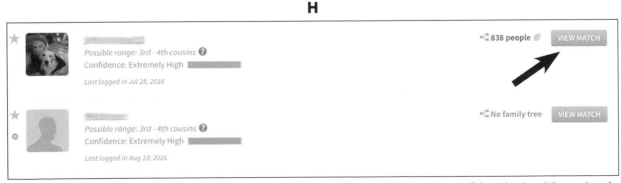

Your DNA results will display the usernames of your matches, plus a possible range of relationship, a confidence level, and the number of people in the match's family tree (if they've uploaded one). Click View Match for more detail.

nected a family tree to their DNA results. If one of your DNA matches has uploaded a family tree, click View Match (image **H**).

This will open a page showing their family tree (in pedigree chart format) as well as a section that shows their surnames that match yours (image **I**). The page showing the DNA match family tree also has an option to view a map and birth locations that are common to both family trees.

For more help tracking your DNA matches, see the DNA Cousin Match Worksheets at the end of this chapter.

New Ancestor Discoveries

This section of your DNA home page is a welcome addition to Ancestry.com. Results appearing in this section are a combination of your DNA testing results,

I

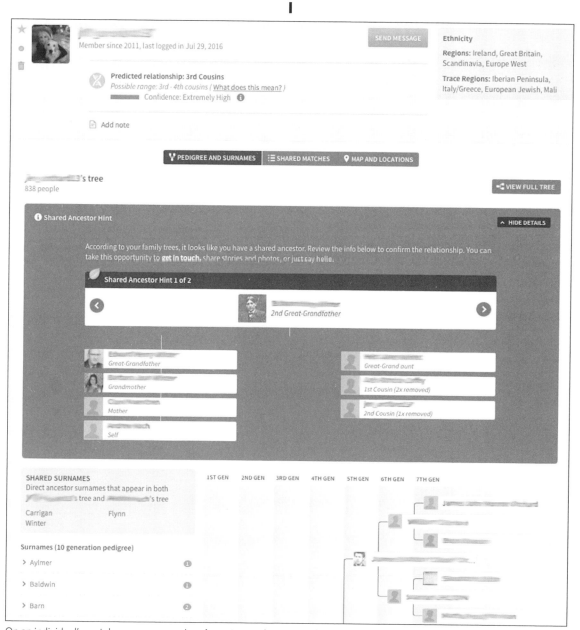

On an individual's match page, you can view Ancestry.com's suggested shared ancestor, plus a link to message the other user, any shared surnames, a combined family tree, and a list of the other user's surnames.

historical information, and results of millions of other Ancestry.com family trees. You actually don't even need to post your own family tree for these results to appear on your page—though I encourage everyone to post a public family tree on Ancestry.com anyway, as not doing so shuts off opportunities to collaborate with other researchers and can be frustrating for other users to see you have either a Private tree or no tree at all.

A New Ancestor Discovery is identified if you share significant DNA with other people in a DNA Circle (described next). This function works from the logic that, if you share DNA with several people who are descended from a common ancestor, you are probably also descended from that same ancestor. Keep in mind, though, that you may not be a descendant of that common ancestor. Still, you can use this information to connect with other people with whom you share DNA and grow your family tree by working with others.

DNA Circles

A DNA Circle comprises people who all share the same ancestor in their family tree and share DNA with at least one other individual in the circle. Circles are created from both your DNA and your family tree.

Ancestry.com uses a five-step process in determining DNA Circles:

1. Compare your DNA with other members' DNA and make matches.
2. Compare your family tree with the family trees of your DNA matches.
3. Determine a "confidence score" for each match, a level of certainty about whether you're actually related to the person as opposed to sharing DNA from a specific region.
4. Add more people to the circle, including people who share an ancestor via a family tree and share DNA with at least one member of the circle. (Note: That member may not be you).
5. Calculate connection levels for everyone in the circle.

Interestingly (as mentioned earlier), you may not have inherited any DNA from some of your ancestors since the pieces of DNA you inherit are mostly random.

CONCLUSION

When you first get your DNA results, it's tempting to jump all over the DNA pages, skimming through the maps and ethnicity estimates. You'll find people in your New Discoveries who are a mystery and you want to contact, and the DNA Circles tool may seem confusing. But instead of jumping right in to interpreting your DNA results, take a look at the exercises that follow to learn how to take a thorough, systematic approach to analyzing your DNA results.

STEP ❶ View your ethnicity estimate and create research questions.

Click See Full Ethnicity Estimate to view a new page with a chart and map. Make sure to click on the + sign next to Trace Regions on the chart to view those regions. You'll see a hodgepodge of regions; some might be well-known, while you may have never heard of others.

Take time to read through the provided information by clicking on each region. For example, this chart showed a Trace Region of Scandinavia, which was a mystery to me. Think of the research challenge this presents!

In a similar way, all the African regions listed here are located on Africa's west coast (the "slave coast"), indicating I have ancestors who were slaves taken to the New World. By the mid-1500s, Spain, Portugal, and England were all exporting slaves from Benin/Togo, which places the date of these ancestors' arrival in America from that era up until the abolition of the slave trade in 1808—a large time frame in which to research, but at least a starting point.

STEP ❷ Create new research goals based on your findings, and use your DNA results as a springboard.

Some of your results, like my Irish estimate, may inspire your inner detective to be more alert to clues to specific clues, such as surnames. For me, it meant going back through the surname list I have and checking if any are on lists of Irish names. For others, like the Benin/Togo connection, you'll have at least the first steps to connecting a slave ancestor to America—a very wide step, I'll admit, but a step nonetheless.

If you took the time to read through the information on each region, you'll also have another list of potential countries of origin. For example, Europe West comprises primarily Belgium, France, Germany, Netherlands, Switzerland, Luxembourg, and Liechtenstein.

❶

Africa		38%
■ Benin/Togo		12%
▨ Ivory Coast/Ghana		8%
■ Cameroon/Congo		7%
⊖ Trace Regions ❷		11%
■ Senegal		5%
■ Africa Southeastern Bantu		4%
■ Nigeria		2%

America		1%
⊖ Trace Regions ❷		1%
■ Native American		1%

Europe		60%
■ Europe West		39%
▨ Great Britain		15%
⊖ Trace Regions ❷		6%
▨ Ireland		4%
■ Scandinavia		2%

❷

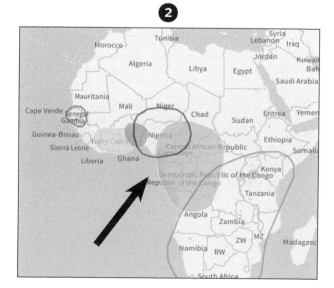

STEP ③ Pick and analyze a New Discovery.

When you click on a name in this section of the site, a pop-up box gives you the opportunity to learn more about the possible ancestor and how you connect to other people in the ancestor's DNA Circle (**A**).

If you click to learn more about the ancestor, you'll be taken to his or her profile page, which contains an Overview, Facts, and Gallery (**B**). The Overview is exactly as you would imagine—a thumbnail sketch of the person's life. Facts include names, dates, and supporting documents. Gallery is a repository for any media attached to the person's profile; this could include census documents, photographs, or videos.

When you click See Your Connection, the system will take you to the ancestor's DNA Circle. It will tell you how many people are in the circle and how many of them match your DNA. If, after analyzing the people in the DNA Circle, you still have no idea of how you connect, click the Send Message icon to contact those whose DNA matches yours—maybe they'll have more information to give you.

A   ❸

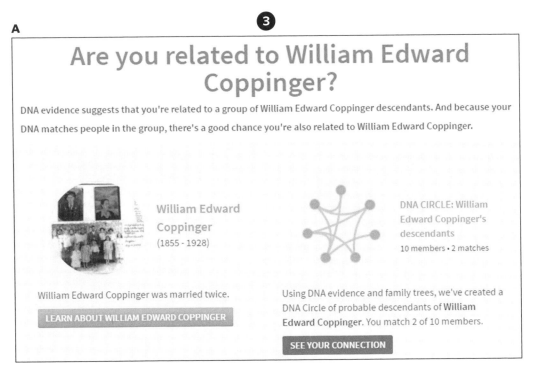

B

STEP ❹ Identify possible relatives with DNA Circle(s).

The next page shows you how many people are in the circle and how many have a DNA match to you (**A**). Keep in mind, these circles will grow and shrink over time; they are constantly in a state of evolution. As you move down the page you'll see the DNA Circle (**B**) with orange lines going from person to person.

The thicker the lines, the stronger the DNA and family tree connections between members. The thin lines indicate weaker DNA and tree connections. When you see a small circle titled as a "family group," the people in that circle are close relatives (mother/daughter, grandmother/granddaughter, etc.).

To the right of the circle you'll see a list of the Circle members and how they might be connected; click another user to see how you might be related (**C**).

A

❹

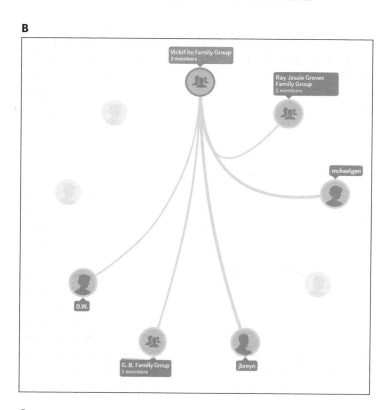

B

C

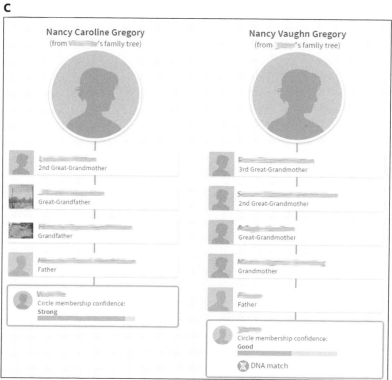

STEP ❶ Review your potential relatives.

Click view all DNA Matches. You could also click on any of the links to the right of the circles; these connect directly to the matches with whom you have shared hints or who are fourth cousins or closer. As noted earlier, matches by default are arranged in order of relationship to you (i.e., those who have a closer relationship to you are at the top of the page).

STEP ❷ Select likely relatives.

Ancestry.com estimates the relationship you and the other user are likely to have. At this point, it's possible to have hundreds of DNA matches. On my profile alone, there are 742 people who are listed as fourth cousins or closer.

The question becomes: Where to begin? My suggestion is to start with second and third cousins. In my case, I have thirteen potential second cousins and thirteen potential third cousins. This means the bulk of my other matches are fourth cousins or greater. (Note: The second cousins have a great-grandparent as their most recent common ancestor; third cousins' most recent ancestor is a great-great-grandparent.)

Of course your ability to match close connections is going to be influenced by 1) whether the matching person has uploaded a family tree and 2) whether the match's family tree is public or private. Of my twenty-six potential second- and third-cousin matches, half of them haven't uploaded a tree.

Once you've completed your research on your closest matches, delve into the matches that go back much further in time.

Once you've found someone of interest, click the star to the left of that person. These "starred match" flags indicate that you want to more closely investigate the user as a possible relative, and starring is a great way to mark interesting matches that you want to easily access later.

❶

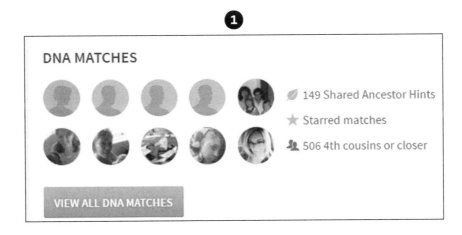

❷

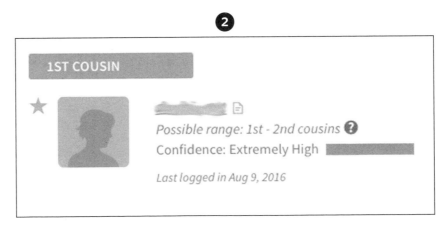

STEP ❸ Contact your match.

The first way to connect to another Ancestry.com member that you match is to click on their name (or initials) from your list of matches. A new page will open with a link to send a message; click the link to open an e-mail box where you can type your message. This e-mail is sent within Ancestry.com's system, meaning other users won't be contacting you via your personal e-mail. When e-mailing a match, I introduce myself and indicate how we're related. I also let my match know what kind of information I have on the family line and that I'm happy to share what I know. Then, I ask any questions I have about the shared family. Once the e-mail is complete, click Send Message.

STEP ❹ Wait for a response.

On the top right of your screen, you'll see a leaf icon that notes the number of hints on your tree and an envelope icon with the number of unread e-mails. Don't be discouraged if your match doesn't respond right away; users might not respond to e-mails on Ancestry.com with the same frequency and urgency as they do other forms of e-mail. If you're lucky, the other user has the answers you need—and maybe will want to team up with you to learn more about your family.

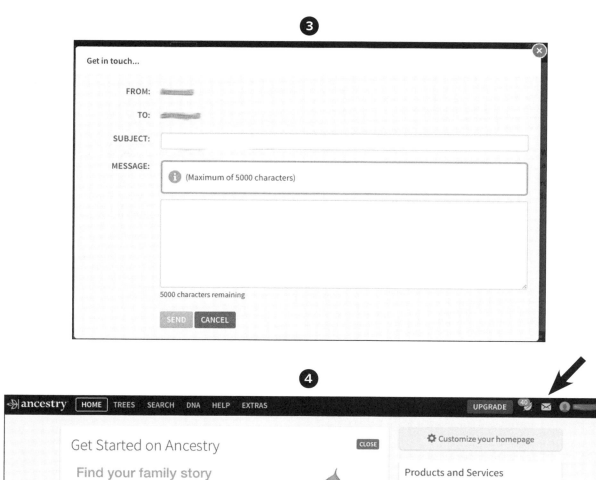

STEP ❶ Identify your goal.

Is there a DNA match whose family tree is populated by several people who aren't in your tree? If so, it's probable that you and your match share a common ancestor, but you may have come down one sibling's line while she came down another. In this instance, you both will have information that's missing from each other's trees, so your goal may be to identify which ancestors you *do* share.

For example, I matched with someone whose name I didn't recognize, but he was listed as a possible third or fourth cousin. By clicking the View Match button, I saw we both belong to the Aaron Hendrickson DNA Circle, meaning Ancestry.com believes we share a common ancestor.

STEP ❷ Gather and analyze data.

I wanted to know which ancestors this match and I share in common. Fortunately, Ancestry.com has put this together as a Shared Ancestor Hint; I scrolled down the page to see it. This showed both my family tree and the tree for my DNA match, emphasizing both of our family lines as they descended from our supposed common ancestor (in this case, two ancestors: Aaron Hendrickson and Polly Moore). I am descended from John Hendrickson, while my DNA match is descended from one of John's sisters (Lucinda).

STEP ❸ Draw your conclusion.

Since I already knew that Lucinda existed, how did this match help my own research? When I clicked on Polly Moore (our shared third great-grandmother), I learned my DNA match has information about Polly that I don't have, including places and dates for her birth, marriage, and death. This information opened a whole new line of research.

In addition, once I clicked through the other names listed (Lucinda, Sarah, etc.), I gained knowledge I could use to untangle several other families I had heard about but weren't sure how they were all connected—all thanks to one DNA match.

❶

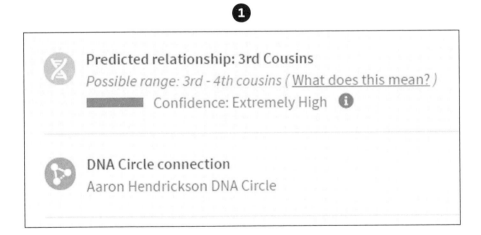

Predicted relationship: 3rd Cousins
Possible range: 3rd - 4th cousins (What does this mean?)
Confidence: Extremely High ⓘ

DNA Circle connection
Aaron Hendrickson DNA Circle

According to your family trees, it looks like you have a shared ancestor. Review the info below to confirm the relationship. You can take this opportunity to **get in touch**, share stories and photos, or just say hello.

Shared Ancestor Hint

Aaron Hendrickson
3rd Great-Grandfather

&

Polly Moore
3rd Great-Grandmother

John Hendrickson
2nd Great-Grandfather

Lucinda Hendrickson
2nd Great-Grand aunt

Great-Grandfather

1st Cousin (3x removed)

Grandfather

2nd Cousin (2x removed)

Father

3rd Cousin (1x removed)

Vicki Noreen Hendrickson
Self

4th Cousin

4th Cousin (1x removed)

Polly Moore
3rd great-grandmother

⇆ View in Tree 📄 View Notes 💬 View Comments ➤ Merge with Duplicate ➕ Save to Tree 🖨 Print 👥 Member Connect

LIFESTORY   FACTS   GALLERY   HINTS ⑤

SHOW ⌄   ➕ ADD ⌄

EDIT

Polly Moore had five sons and 10 daughters with Aaron Hendrickson between 1816 and 1839.

You • • • John Hendrickson — Polly Moore
+ 14 Children ⌄   Aaron Hendrickson

➤ Take the time to explore your DNA matches, particularly those that are third cousins and closer. See the Relationship Chart for how to determine family relationships.

➤ Check the thickness of the orange line in your DNA Circles, as a thin line connecting you to someone in your circle represents a more distant relative.

➤ Avoid making assumptions based on surnames, as a surname matching a more distant DNA match may be coincidental rather than evidential.

➤ Contact people who have made their trees private or who have not uploaded a tree. While they may be hesitant to share their family tree information with you, it's worth helping them understand the value in sharing a family tree with other researchers.

➤ Review your DNA results often to see any changes in your results or connections, as Ancestry.com is constantly refining its DNA results. For example, as reported DNA matches become more accurate, some of the less-accurate ones will be removed from your connections.

➤ Keep inheritance patterns in mind. You inherit roughly half of your DNA from each of your parents, your parents inherit half from each of their parents, and so on. No parent can select which DNA they pass on, meaning that over time, you may not share detectable amounts of DNA with an ancestor even though you are genealogically related.

RELATIONSHIP CHART

Instructions:

1. Identify the most recent common ancestor of the two individuals with the unknown relationship.

2. Determine the common ancestor's relationship to each person (for example, grandparent or great-grandparent).

3. In the topmost row of the chart, find the common ancestor's relationship to cousin number one. In the far-left column, find the common ancestor's relationship to cousin number two.

4. Trace the row and column from step 3. The square where they meet shows the two individuals' relationship.

THE MOST RECENT COMMON ANCESTOR IS COUSIN NUMBER ONE'S ...

	parent	grandparent	great-grandparent	great-great-grandparent	third-great-grandparent	fourth-great-grandparent	fifth-great-grandparent	sixth-great-grandparent
parent	siblings	nephew or niece	grandnephew or -niece	great-grandnephew or -niece	great-great-grandnephew or -niece	third-great-grandnephew or -niece	fourth-great-grandnephew or -niece	fifth-great-grandnephew or -niece
grandparent	nephew or niece	first cousins	first cousins once removed	first cousins twice removed	first cousins three times removed	first cousins four times removed	first cousins five times removed	first cousins six times removed
great-grandparent	grandnephew or -niece	first cousins once removed	second cousins	second cousins once removed	second cousins twice removed	second cousins three times removed	second cousins four times removed	second cousins five times removed
great-great-grandparent	great-grandnephew or -niece	first cousins twice removed	second cousins once removed	third cousins	third cousins once removed	third cousins twice removed	third cousins three times removed	third cousins four times removed
third-great-grandparent	great-great-grandnephew or -niece	first cousins three times removed	second cousins twice removed	third cousins once removed	fourth cousins	fourth cousins once removed	fourth cousins twice removed	fourth cousins three times removed
fourth-great-grandparent	third-great-grandnephew or -niece	first cousins four times removed	second cousins three times removed	third cousins twice removed	fourth cousins once removed	fifth cousins	fifth cousins once removed	fifth cousins twice removed
fifth-great-grandparent	fourth-great-grandnephew or -niece	first cousins five times removed	second cousins four times removed	third cousins three times removed	fourth cousins twice removed	fifth cousins once removed	sixth cousins	sixth cousins once removed

... THE MOST RECENT COMMON ANCESTOR IS COUSIN NUMBER TWO'S

QUICK GUIDE: ETHNICITY ESTIMATE GLOBAL REGIONS

AncestryDNA divides the world into several geographic regions and subregions that its analysis tool uses to determine your ethnicity estimate. These regions and subregions are listed below. Note that this categorization system may have changed since this book's publication.

Africa

Africa
- Africa North
- Africa Southeastern Bantu
- Benin/Togo
- Ivory Coast/Ghana
- Nigeria

Africa South-Central
- Cameroon/Congo
- Mali
- Senegal

Native American

Asia

Asia
- Asia South
- Asia East
- Asia Central

West Asia
- Middle East
- Caucasus

Europe
- Great Britain
- Europe West
- Ireland
- Italy/Greece
- Scandinavia
- Iberian Peninsula
- Europe East
- European Jewish
- Finland/Northwest Russia

Oceania

Pacific Islander
- Melanesia
- Polynesia

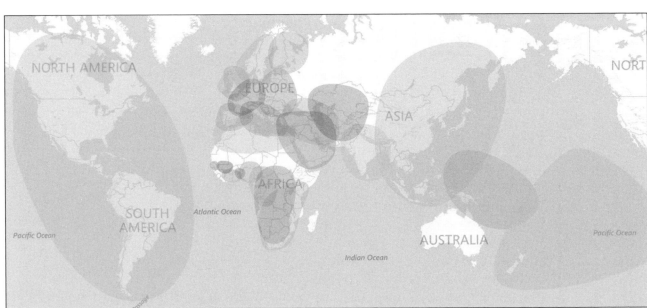

Image courtesy blogs.ancestry.com

Adapted from *The Family Tree Guide to DNA Testing and Genetic Genealogy*. Copyright © 2016 Blaine T. Bettinger

BASIC DNA COUSIN MATCH WORKSHEET

Test results identify "cousin matches"—that is, people who share a portion of their DNA with you. You'll use online tools to identify additional matches who tested with other companies. In general, the more DNA you share, the closer your biological relationship. For each cousin match, your results will specify the percentage match, the measurement of your longest shared DNA segment (expressed in "centimorgans") and the relationship (second cousin, fourth cousin, etc.). Using this data, you'll then collaborate with your cousins to identify your common ancestor or family line. It's helpful to keep track of your matches in one place to spot patterns and clues, and note theories, objectives and next steps.

Percentage match	Centimorgans (cM)	Relationship	Notes

DETAILED MATCH RELATIONSHIP WORKSHEET

Use this tracker to note key clues that could help you determine how you and your genetic cousins are related.

	Username of match	Estimated relationship	Contact info (if known)	Shared ancestral places	Match's Ancestors from Shared Places
1					
2					
3					
4					
5					
6					
7					
8					
9					
10					

DETAILED MATCH RELATIONSHIP WORKSHEET

	Username of match	Shared surnames	Match's relative(s) with that surname (and relationship to user)	Shared ethnic origins	Notes
1					
2					
3					
4					
5					
6					
7					
8					
9					
10					

ACCOUNT INFO AND QUICK LINKS

This workbook has discussed how to search each of Ancestry.com's categories of records, plus how to understand and use your AncestryDNA results in your research. Now, we'll pan out and give you tools for using the whole Ancestry.com website.

Store your account information (username, password, e-mail address, etc.) and notes about your family trees and AncestryDNA tests in the table below, then see the sections on quick links and keyboard shortcuts to more easily navigate the site.

ACCOUNT INFORMATION

Username		
E-mail address		
Password		
Account type	☐ Basic (free) ☐ U.S. Discovery ☐ World Explorer ☐ All Access	Subscription expires: Payment method: ☐ Monthly ☐ Semiannually
Family trees		Notes:
AncestryDNA tests		Notes:

ANCESTRY.COM QUICK LINKS

Ancestry.com's Quick Links module lets you bookmark web links that you'd like to save for future reference, both those on Ancestry.com and those at other genealogy websites such as FamilySearch.org <www.familysearch.org> and USGenWeb <www.usgenweb.org>.

To add a Quick Links module to your home page, click the Customize Your Homepage link in the upper right corner of your home page. Select Quick Links from the list of available modules, then click the Add to Your Homepage button.

While on your Ancestry.com home page, you can create a Quick Link by clicking the Add a Link button located at the top of the My Quick Links module. Then type in the website address (URL) of a favorite site or page, then name the link. Click Save, and the site will appear in your list of Quick Links.

Here are a few Ancestry.com links you may want to save in the My Quick Links module:

- Blog <blogs.ancestry.com/ancestry>
- Card Catalog <search.ancestry.com/search/CardCatalog.aspx>
- Facebook <www.facebook.com/Ancestry.com>
- Family History Wiki <www.ancestry.com/wiki>
- How-to videos on YouTube <www.youtube.com/user/Ancestrycom>
- Learning Center <ancestry.com/cs/HelpAndAdviceUS>
- Message Boards <boards.ancestry.com>
- My Account <secure.ancestry.com/myaccount>
- News and updated collections <www.ancestry.com/cs/recent-collections>
- Search <search.ancestry.com>
- Support <help.ancestry.com>

You can also add quick links for other websites, such as FamilyTreeMagazine.com <www.familytreemagazine.com> and FamilySearch.org <www.familysearch.org>. See a list of non-Ancestry.com resources for each type of record at <ftu.familytreemagazine.com/unofficial-ancestry-workbook>.

My Quick Links [ADD A LINK]

- Ancestry Card Catalog
- Birth, Marriage & Death Records
- U.S. Census Records
- Immigration & Emigration Records
- Military Collection
- Family Tree Magazine website
- Family Tree University

Ancestry.com allows you to save shortcuts called Quick Links, making your most-used resources more accessible.

ANCESTRY.COM SHORTCUT KEYS

Shortcut keys (aka "hot keys") are keyboard strokes that you can use to save time when searching and viewing results on Ancestry.com. Here's a look at the most common keyboard shortcuts you'll use. (Note: PC users need to hit the Ctrl button along with the shortcut key, and Mac users may need to hit the Command button along with the shortcut key.)

Shortcut	Purpose
n	Launches a new search by opening a new search form
r	Refines your search (Note: It will launch a search form that's pre-populated using the data you just searched; it also enables you to edit information in a search form without using the back keys or the Edit link.)
p	Previews current record in search result
>	Highlights next record
<	Highlights previous record

RESEARCH CHECKLISTS AND WORKSHEETS

So far, this workbook has contained worksheets for finding individual kinds of records. These can be useful as you conduct specific research, but Ancestry.com users can also benefit from more general research forms and checklists that can help you organize your research finds. This section contains several worksheets that you can use to keep track of your research, whether on Ancestry.com or on other sites.

In this section, you'll find:

- **Your Ancestry.com Search Worksheet:** Make your own versions of this workbook's exercises and apply them to your personal research goals.

- **Five-Generation Ancestor Chart:** Track your ancestors back to your great-great-grandparents.

- **Family Group Sheet:** Record information about a couple/an entire family unit.

- **Research Checklists for Ancestors:** Identify records resources to search as you research US, UK, and Canadian ancestors.

- **Records Checklists for Vital Information:** Discover sources to consult when looking for your ancestor's birth, marriage, and death information.

- **Collections to Search Worksheet:** Target your search by identifying the Ancestry.com records collection most likely to give you success.

Like the other worksheets in this book, you can find downloadable versions of these forms at <ftu.familytreemagazine.com/unofficial-ancestry-workbook>. You can also find more research forms online at <www.familytreemagazine.com/freeforms>.

EXERCISE Your Ancestry.com Search Worksheet

Apply the example searches in this workbook to your own family research. Fill in your search's title and a research goal/problem, then add steps from the sample exercises. Once you've begun your research, add your results and any notes.

RESEARCH GOAL: _____

STEP ❶ _____

_____

RESULTS/NOTES: _____

_____

_____

_____

_____

STEP ❷ _____

_____

RESULTS/NOTES: _____

_____

_____

_____

_____

STEP ❸ _____

_____

RESULTS/NOTES: _____

_____

_____

_____

_____

STEP ❹ _____

_____

RESULTS/NOTES: _____

_____

_____

_____

_____

Fill in your search's title and a research goal/problem, then add in your own steps to solve it. Once you've begun your research, add your results and any notes.

RESEARCH GOAL: _____

STEP ❶ _____

RESULTS/NOTES: _____

STEP ❷ _____

RESULTS/NOTES: _____

STEP ❸ _____

RESULTS/NOTES: _____

STEP ❹ _____

RESULTS/NOTES: _____

Fill in your search's title and a research goal/problem, then add in your own steps to solve it.
Once you've begun your research, add your results and any notes.

RESEARCH GOAL: _____

STEP ❶ _____

_____

RESULTS/NOTES: _____

_____

_____

_____

_____

_____

STEP ❷ _____

_____

RESULTS/NOTES: _____

_____

_____

_____

_____

_____

STEP ❸ _____

_____

RESULTS/NOTES: _____

_____

_____

_____

_____

_____

STEP ❹ _____

_____

RESULTS/NOTES: _____

_____

_____

_____

_____

_____

Your Ancestry.com Search Worksheet

Fill in your search's title and a research goal/problem, then add in your own steps to solve it. Once you've begun your research, add your results and any notes.

RESEARCH GOAL: _____

STEP ❶ _____

_____

RESULTS/NOTES: _____

_____

_____

_____

_____

STEP ❷ _____

_____

RESULTS/NOTES: _____

_____

_____

_____

_____

STEP ❸ _____

_____

RESULTS/NOTES: _____

_____

_____

_____

_____

STEP ❹ _____

_____

RESULTS/NOTES: _____

_____

_____

_____

_____

FIVE-GENERATION ANCESTOR CHART

Chart # ___
1 on this chart = ___ on chart # ___

see chart #

1

birth date and place

marriage date and place

death date and place

spouse

2

birth date and place

marriage date and place

death date and place

3

birth date and place

death date and place

4

birth date and place

marriage date and place

death date and place

5

birth date and place

death date and place

6

birth date and place

marriage date and place

death date and place

7

birth date and place

death date and place

8

birth date and place

marriage date and place

death date and place

9

birth date and place

death date and place

10

birth date and place

marriage date and place

death date and place

11

birth date and place

death date and place

12

birth date and place

marriage date and place

death date and place

13

birth date and place

death date and place

14

birth date and place

marriage date and place

death date and place

15

birth date and place

death date and place

16

17

18

19

20

21

22

23

24

25

26

27

28

29

30

31

©2016 FAMILY TREE MAGAZINE

FAMILY GROUP SHEET OF THE

_____FAMILY

Husband   Source #

Full name _____ _____

Birth date _____Place _____ _____

Marriage date _____Place _____ _____

Death date_____Place _____ _____

    Burial_____ _____

His father _____ _____

His mother with maiden name _____ _____

Wife

Full name _____ _____

Birth date _____Place _____ _____

Death date_____Place _____ _____

    Burial_____ _____

Her father _____ _____

Her mother with maiden name _____ _____

Other Spouses

Full name _____ _____

    Marriage date and place _____ _____

Full name _____ _____

    Marriage date and place _____ _____

Children of this marriage	Birth date and place	Death and burial dates and places	Spouse and marriage date and place

RESEARCH CHECKLIST FOR US ANCESTORS

Federal census

Search each US census taken during your ancestor's lifetime. Due to the different information collected from census to census, search each census collection individually to utilize search parameters available only for that census. Federal censuses were taken every ten years. Currently available collections include censuses from 1790 to 1940. (Note: The 1890 census contains only a fragment of the records due to water damage following a fire.)

☐ 1940   ☐ 1880   ☐ 1830
☐ 1930   ☐ 1870   ☐ 1820
☐ 1920   ☐ 1860   ☐ 1810
☐ 1910   ☐ 1850   ☐ 1800
☐ 1900   ☐ 1840   ☐ 1790
☐ 1890

Vital records

Drill down to the records relating specifically to your ancestor's place of birth, marriage, and death. Use the search filters to narrow by collection or the Card Catalog to find individual collections to search. Start with death records and work your way backwards. Death records often contain more information that will help you than other vital records.

BIRTH AND DEATH RECORDS
☐ birth certificates
☐ death certificates
☐ Social Security Death Index
☐ obituaries and death announcements in newspapers
☐ burial and grave records
☐ wills
☐ probate court records

MARRIAGE AND DIVORCE RECORDS
☐ marriage bonds, licenses, and certificates
☐ engagement, wedding, or anniversary announcements in newspapers
☐ divorce records

CHURCH RECORDS
☐ baptism/christening record
☐ marriage banns/records
☐ burial records

Other records

Many other records collections may have information on your ancestors or the areas and time periods in which they lived.

MILITARY
☐ draft, enlistment, and service records
☐ soldier, veteran, and prisoner rolls and lists
☐ pension records
☐ regimental histories

IMMIGRATION AND TRAVEL
☐ passenger and ship crew lists
☐ border crossing records and passports
☐ naturalization records
☐ federal census records

PUBLICATIONS
☐ newspapers
☐ genealogical periodicals
☐ compiled genealogies (family histories, biographies)
☐ American Genealogical-Biographical Index
☐ oral histories and interviews
☐ local and county histories
☐ church histories
☐ school lists and yearbooks
☐ city and area directories
☐ telephone directories
☐ professional and organizational directories
☐ maps, atlases, and gazetteers

LAND RECORDS
☐ deeds
☐ bounty land warrants
☐ homestead records
☐ land grants and patents

LEGAL RECORDS
☐ tax lists
☐ criminal lists/criminal case files
☐ convict/prisoner records
☐ court records
☐ guardianship papers

NON-FEDERAL CENSUS RECORDS
☐ state and local censuses
☐ voter registration lists

RESEARCH CHECKLIST FOR CANADIAN ANCESTORS

Census records

Ancestry.com's Canadian census collection includes indexes and images to Canadian censuses for every decade from 1851 to 1911, and censuses of Manitoba, Saskatchewan, and Alberta from 1906 and 1916. The censuses for the years listed below are for the entire country, unless otherwise indicated.

- ☐ 1825 (Lower Canada)
- ☐ 1842 (Canada East)
- ☐ 1851 (Canada East, Canada West, New Brunswick, Nova Scotia)
- ☐ 1861
- ☐ 1871
- ☐ 1881
- ☐ 1891
- ☐ 1901
- ☐ 1906 (Manitoba, Saskatchewan, Alberta)
- ☐ 1911
- ☐ 1916 (Manitoba, Saskatchewan, Alberta)
- ☐ 1921

Vital records

Canadian vital records are most often found in collections by province.

- ☐ church records
- ☐ marriage records
- ☐ death records
- ☐ birth records
- ☐ christening records
- ☐ burial indexes

Other records

Many other records collections may have information on your Canadian ancestors or the areas and time periods in which they lived. Look for the following types of records on your ancestors.

MILITARY RECORDS

- ☐ service and pension records
- ☐ death or casualty lists
- ☐ draft or enlistment records

PUBLICATIONS

- ☐ newspapers
- ☐ maps, atlases, and gazetteers
- ☐ local histories
- ☐ *The Canada Directory* (directory of professionals and businessmen)
- ☐ school student and alumni lists
- ☐ telephone directories

RESEARCH CHECKLIST FOR UK ANCESTORS

Census records

United Kingdom census information varies by year. On Ancestry.com, you'll find census records from England, Scotland, Wales, the Channel Islands, and the Isle of Man, covering every decade from 1841 to 1911.

- ☐ 1841
- ☐ 1851
- ☐ 1861
- ☐ 1871
- ☐ 1881
- ☐ 1891
- ☐ 1901
- ☐ 1911

Vital records

You'll often find England and Wales in collections separate from Scotland and Ireland. Countries covered are Channel Islands, England, Isle of Man, Northern Ireland, Scotland, and Wales. Collections include

- ☐ baptisms
- ☐ marriage banns
- ☐ burials
- ☐ civil registration records (birth, marriage, or death certificates)

Other records

Many other records collections may have information on your UK ancestors or the areas and time periods in which they lived. Look for the following records on your ancestors.

MILITARY RECORDS

- ☐ service and pension records
- ☐ prisoners of war lists
- ☐ casualty lists
- ☐ grave registers

PUBLICATIONS AND HISTORIES

- ☐ newspapers
- ☐ maps, atlases, and gazetteers
- ☐ local histories
- ☐ photos (such as coats of arms)
- ☐ professional and organizational directories
- ☐ city and county directories
- ☐ telephone directories
- ☐ school student and alumni lists

LEGAL RECORDS

- ☐ wills
- ☐ probate records

RECORDS CHECKLIST: BIRTH INFORMATION

Ancestor's name	
Birthplace (if known)	
Places of residence (clues to birthplace and possible locations for records)	
Other known details	

First, search for ...

BIRTH CERTIFICATES, REGISTRATIONS
- ☐ home
- ☐ city, county and state record offices

BABY BOOKS, ANNOUNCEMENTS, MEMENTOS
- ☐ home

FAMILY BIBLE, PHOTOS, HEIRLOOMS
- ☐ home
- ☐ other family members
- ☐ online family trees, websites

BAPTISM, CONFIRMATION, OTHER RELIGIOUS RECORDS
- ☐ home
- ☐ church

US CENSUS INFORMATION
- ☐ agriculture schedules
- ☐ Civil War veterans schedules
- ☐ defective, dependent and delinquent schedules
- ☐ federal population schedules for years
- ☐ manufacturing/industry schedules
- ☐ mortality schedules
- ☐ American Indian special censuses
- ☐ school censuses
- ☐ slave schedules
- ☐ social statistics schedules
- ☐ state and local censuses

BIRTH ANNOUNCEMENTS
- ☐ newspapers

Then, search for ...

DEATH CERTIFICATES
- ☐ home
- ☐ city, county, state record offices

FUNERAL PROGRAM, GUEST BOOK, MEMORIAL CARD
- ☐ home

FUNERAL RECORD
- ☐ funeral home
- ☐ church and minister's records

CEMETERY RECORDS, GRAVESTONE INSCRIPTIONS

WILLS, PROBATE FILES, GUARDIANSHIPS, CUSTODY RECORDS
- ☐ city, county, state record offices

OBITUARIES
- ☐ newspapers and professional journals
- ☐ club and organization newsletters

LAND AND PROPERTY RECORDS
- ☐ city, county, federal records

SCHOOL RECORDS, YEARBOOKS
- ☐ school libraries

MILITARY RECORDS
- ☐ local newspapers
- ☐ military records

EMPLOYMENT
- ☐ professional licenses and organizations
- ☐ railroad, mining, factory, business records
- ☐ insurance records

Adapted from *How to Archive Family Keepsakes*. Copyright © 2012 Denise May Levenick

RECORDS CHECKLIST: MARRIAGE INFORMATION

Couple's names	
Place of marriage (if known)	
Places of residence (clues to place of marriage and possible locations for records)	
Other known details	

First, search for ...

CEMETERY RECORDS, GRAVESTONE INSCRIPTIONS

☐ cemeteries

☐ gravestones

ENGAGEMENT AND MARRIAGE ANNOUNCEMENTS

☐ newspapers

FAMILY BIBLE, PHOTOS, HEIRLOOMS

☐ home

☐ other family members

☐ online family trees, websites

MARRIAGE CERTIFICATES, BONDS, LICENSES

☐ home

☐ city, county, state record offices

MARRIAGE BANNS, RECORDS

☐ church and minister's records

OBITUARIES

☐ newspapers

☐ professional journals

☐ club and organization newsletters

US CENSUS INFORMATION

☐ agriculture schedules (1850, 1860, 1870, 1880)

☐ Civil War veterans schedules (1890)

☐ Defective, dependent, and delinquent (DDD) schedules (1880)

☐ federal population schedules for years

☐ manufacturing/industry schedules (1810, 1820, 1850, 1860, 1870, 1880)

☐ mortality schedules (1850, 1860, 1870, 1880)

☐ American Indian special censuses

☐ school censuses

☐ slave schedules (1850, 1860)

☐ social statistics schedules

☐ state and local censuses

WEDDING ALBUMS

☐ home

Then, search for ...

COURT RECORDS

☐ city, county, federal records

LAND AND PROPERTY RECORDS

☐ city, county, federal records

MILITARY RECORDS

☐ local newspapers

☐ military records (see Military Checklist)

WILLS, PROBATE FILES, GUARDIANSHIPS, CUSTODY RECORDS

☐ city, county, state record offices

Adapted from *How to Archive Family Keepsakes*. Copyright © 2012 Denise May Levenick

RECORDS CHECKLIST: DEATH INFORMATION

Ancestor's name	
Place of death (if known)	
Places of residence (clues to place of death and possible locations for records)	
Other known details	

First, search for ...

CEMETERY RECORDS, GRAVESTONE INSCRIPTIONS

☐ cemeteries

☐ gravestones

DEATH CERTIFICATES

☐ home

☐ city, county, state record offices

FUNERAL OR MEMORIAL PROGRAM, GUEST BOOK, MEMORIAL CARD

☐ home

FAMILY BIBLE, PHOTOS, HEIRLOOMS

☐ home

☐ other family members

☐ online family trees, websites

OBITUARIES

☐ professional journals

☐ club and organization newsletters

US CENSUS INFORMATION

☐ agriculture schedules (1850, 1860, 1870, 1880)

☐ Civil War veterans schedules (1890)

☐ defective, dependent and delinquent ("DDD") schedules (1880)

☐ federal population schedules for years

☐ manufacturing/industry schedules (1810, 1820, 1880)

☐ mortality schedules (1850, 1860, 1870, 1880)

☐ American Indian special censuses

☐ school censuses

☐ slave schedules (1850, 1860)

☐ social statistics schedules

☐ state and local censuses

RETIREMENT AND PENSION RECORDS

☐ Social Security Death Index

☐ Railroad Retirement Board

☐ other retirement records

Then, search for ...

COURT RECORDS

☐ city, county, federal records

EMPLOYMENT

☐ professional licenses and organizations

☐ railroad, mining, factory, business records

☐ insurance records

FUNERAL RECORD

☐ funeral home

☐ church and minister's records

LAND AND PROPERTY RECORDS

☐ city, county, federal records

MILITARY RECORDS

☐ local newspapers

☐ military records

Adapted from *How to Archive Family Keepsakes*. Copyright © 2012 Denise May Levenick

COLLECTIONS TO SEARCH WORKSHEET

Ancestry.com has more than thirty-two thousand records collections in its database, and knowing which collections to search can be difficult. Check out this list of popular records collections below, then record information about the collections you want to search in the chart.

Census

☐ United States Federal Collection, 1790-1940 (fifteen separate collections)
☐ U.S., Selected Federal Census Non-Population Schedules, 1850-1880
☐ U.S., Indian Census Rolls, 1885-1940
☐ England Census, 1851-1911 (nine separate collections)

Birth, Marriage & Death

☐ U.S., Find a Grave Index, 1600s-Current
☐ U.S., Social Security Death Index, 1935-2014
☐ U.S. and International Marriage Records, 1560-1900
☐ England, Select Births and Christenings, 1538-1975
☐ England, Civil Registration Death Index, 1916-2007
☐ Scotland, Select Births and Baptisms, 1564-1950
☐ Germany, Select Births and Baptisms, 1558-1898 (in German)

Military

☐ U.S., Revolutionary War Pension and Bound-Land Warrant Application Files, 1800-1900
☐ U.S., Sons of the American Revolution Membership Applications, 1889-1970
☐ U.S. Civil War Draft Registration Records, 1863-1865
☐ U.S. Civil War Soldiers, 1861-1865
☐ U.S., Civil War Pension Index: General Index to Pension Files, 1861-1934
☐ U.S. World War I Draft Registration Cards, 1917-1918
☐ U.S. World War II Draft Registration Cards, 1942
☐ U.S. World War II Army Enlistment Records, 1938-1946
☐ U.S. Marine Corp Muster Rolls. 1798-1958
☐ U.S. Veteran Gravesites, ca. 1775-2006

Immigration

☐ New York, Passenger Lists, 1820-1957
☐ New York, Passenger and Immigration Lists, 1820-1850
☐ Baltimore Passenger Lists, 1820-1964
☐ New Orleans, Passenger Lists, 1813-1963
☐ U.S. Naturalization Record Indexes, 1791-1992 (Indexed in World Archives Project)
☐ U.S. and Canada, Passenger and Immigration Lists Index, 1500s-1900s
☐ U.S., Border Crossings from Canada to U.S., 1895-1956
☐ Border Crossings: From Mexico to U.S., 1895-1964
☐ U.S. Passport Applications, 1795-1925
☐ Hamburg Passenger Lists, 1850-1934 (in German)
☐ Canadian Passenger Lists, 1865-1935

Historical Maps, Images, and Publications

☐ U.S., School Yearbooks, 1880-2012
☐ Historical Newspapers, Birth, Marriage & Death Announcements, 1851-2003
☐ U.S. Map Collection, 1513-1990
☐ Public Member Photos & Scanned Documents
☐ Historic Catalogs of Sears, Roebuck and Co., 1896-1993
☐ U.S. Obituary Collection, 1930-2015
☐ Passenger Ships and Images
☐ U.S., Historical Postcards
☐ Meyers Gazetteer of the German Empire (in German)

Social History

☐ Public Member Trees
☐ Public Member Stories
☐ U.S. City Directories, 1822-1995
☐ U.S. Public Records Index, 1950-1993, Volume 1
☐ U.S. Public Records Index, 1950-1993, Volume 2
☐ U.S., IRS Tax Assessment Lists, 1862-1918
☐ U.S. General Land Office Records, 1796-1907
☐ U.S., Quaker Meeting Records, 1681-1935
☐ Ireland, Griffith's Valuation, 1847-1864

COLLECTIONS TO SEARCH WORKSHEET

Collection name and URL	Record type	Coverage	Notes
	☐ Census ☐ Historical Images ☐ Birth/Baptismal ☐ Publications ☐ Marriage ☐ Directories ☐ Death/Burial ☐ Tax/Estate ☐ Military ☐ Land/Property ☐ Immigration ☐ Other social history ☐ Maps ☐ Other: _____		
	☐ Census ☐ Historical Images ☐ Birth/Baptismal ☐ Publications ☐ Marriage ☐ Directories ☐ Death/Burial ☐ Tax/Estate ☐ Military ☐ Land/Property ☐ Immigration ☐ Other social history ☐ Maps ☐ Other: _____		
	☐ Census ☐ Historical Images ☐ Birth/Baptismal ☐ Publications ☐ Marriage ☐ Directories ☐ Death/Burial ☐ Tax/Estate ☐ Military ☐ Land/Property ☐ Immigration ☐ Other social history ☐ Maps ☐ Other: _____		
	☐ Census ☐ Historical Images ☐ Birth/Baptismal ☐ Publications ☐ Marriage ☐ Directories ☐ Death/Burial ☐ Tax/Estate ☐ Military ☐ Land/Property ☐ Immigration ☐ Other social history ☐ Maps ☐ Other: _____		
	☐ Census ☐ Historical Images ☐ Birth/Baptismal ☐ Publications ☐ Marriage ☐ Directories ☐ Death/Burial ☐ Tax/Estate ☐ Military ☐ Land/Property ☐ Immigration ☐ Other social history ☐ Maps ☐ Other: _____		
	☐ Census ☐ Historical Images ☐ Birth/Baptismal ☐ Publications ☐ Marriage ☐ Directories ☐ Death/Burial ☐ Tax/Estate ☐ Military ☐ Land/Property ☐ Immigration ☐ Other social history ☐ Maps ☐ Other: _____		

CENSUS ABSTRACT FORMS

As I discussed in chapter 2, census records are the first (and often, most important) resources that genealogists consult. As a result, you'll find yourself reviewing federal census records early and often in your research, and having to re-find your ancestor's entry each time can be a pain.

While census records are most notable for providing your ancestors' names, ages, and addresses, they also provide a wealth of information about your ancestors' lives—and you should always look at whatever information the census provides. Each federal census asked slightly different questions, providing new and unique avenues of research.

This section provides census abstract forms that you can use to record individual federal census entries from 1790 to 1940 (minus the 1890 census, most of which has been destroyed). By having an at-a-glance abstract, you can easily access your ancestor's entry (and *just* your ancestor's entry).

You can download a Word version of these forms at <ftu.familytreemagazine.com/unofficial-ancestry-workbook>. You can type directly into these files as you transcribe census forms, or print them and fill them out by hand. *Family Tree Magazine* has also created free templates that you can download online at <www.familytreemagazine.com/info/censusforms>.

1790 US CENSUS

Census question	Answer
Township or community	
County	
State	
Enumerator	
Enumeration date	
Enumeration district number	
Name of head of family	
Free white males 16 years of age and upwards, including heads of families	
Free white males under 16 years of age	
Free white females, including heads of families	
All other free persons	
Slaves	

1800 US CENSUS

Census question	Answer
Township or community	
County	
State	
Name of institution	
Name of incorporated place	
Enumeration date	
Enumerator	
Ward of city	
Supervisor's district	
Enumerator's district	
Written page number	
Printed page number	

Census question	Answer
Name of head of family	
Free white males under 10 years of age	
Free white males 10-16 years of age	
Free white males 16-26 years of age	
Free white males 26-45 years of age	
Free white males 45 and over	
Free white females under 10 years of age	
Free white females 10-16 years of age	
Free white females 16-26 years of age	
Free white females 26-45 years of age	
Free white females 45 and over	
All other free persons except Indians not taxed	
Slaves	

1810 US CENSUS

Census question	Answer
Township or community	
County	
State	
Name of institution	
Name of incorporated place	
Enumeration date	
Enumerator	
Ward of city	
Supervisor's district	
Enumerator's district	
Written page number	
Printed page number	

Census question	Answer
Name of head of family	
Free white males under 10 years of age	
Free white males 10–16 years of age	
Free white males 16–26 years of age	
Free white males 26–45 years of age	
Free white males 45 and over	
Free white females under 10 years of age	
Free white females 10–16 years of age	
Free white females 16–26 years of age	
Free white females 26–45 years of age	
Free white females 45 and over	
All other free persons except Indians not taxed	
Slaves	

1820 US CENSUS

Census question	Answer
Township or community	
County	
State	
Name of institution	
Name of incorporated place	
Enumeration date	
Enumerator	
Ward of city	
Supervisor's district	
Enumerator's district	
Written page number	
Printed page number	

Census question	Answer
Name of head of family	
Free white males under 10 years of age	
Free white males 10-16 years of age	
Free white males 16-26 years of age	
Free white males 26-45 years of age	
Free white males 45 and over	
Free white females under 10 years of age	
Free white females 10-16 years of age	
Free white females 16-26 years of age	
Free white females 26-45 years of age	
Free white females 45 and over	
Foreigners, not naturalized	
Agriculture	
Commerce	
Manufacturing	
Free colored males	
Free colored females	
All other persons	
Slaves	

1830 US CENSUS

Census question	Answer
Township or community	
County	
State	
Name of institution	
Name of incorporated place	
Enumeration date	

Census question	Answer
Enumerator	
Ward of city	
Supervisor's district	
Enumerator's district	
Written page number	
Printed page number	
Name of head of family	
Free white males under 5 years of age	
Free white males 5–10 years of age	
Free white males 10–15 years of age	
Free white males 15–20 years of age	
Free white males 20–30 years of age	
Free white males 30–40 years of age	
Free white males 40–50 years of age	
Free white males 50–60 years of age	
Free white males 60–70 years of age	
Free white males 70–80 years of age	
Free white males 80–90 years of age	
Free white males 90–100 years of age	
Free white females under 5 years of age	
Free white females 5–10 years of age	
Free white females 10–15 years of age	
Free white females 15–20 years of age	
Free white females 20–30 years of age	
Free white females 30–40 years of age	
Free white females 40–50 years of age	
Free white females 50–60 years of age	
Free white females 60–70 years of age	

Census question	Answer
Free white females 70–80 years of age	
Free white females 80–90 years of age	
Free white females 90–100 years of age	
Slaves	
Free colored people	
Deaf and dumb	
Blind	
Foreigners, not naturalized	

1840 US CENSUS

Census question	Answer
Township or community	
County	
State	
Name of institution	
Name of incorporated place	
Enumeration date	
Enumerator	
Ward of city	
Supervisor's district	
Enumerator's district	
Written page number	
Printed page number	
Name of head of family	
Free white males under 5 years of age	
Free white males 5–10 years of age	
Free white males 10–15 years of age	
Free white males 15–20 years of age	

Census question	Answer
Free white males 20–30 years of age	
Free white males 30–40 years of age	
Free white males 40–50 years of age	
Free white males 50–60 years of age	
Free white males 60–70 years of age	
Free white males 70–80 years of age	
Free white males 80–90 years of age	
Free white males 90–100 years of age	
Free white females under 5 years of age	
Free white females 5–10 years of age	
Free white females 10–15 years of age	
Free white females 15–20 years of age	
Free white females 20–30 years of age	
Free white females 30–40 years of age	
Free white females 40–50 years of age	
Free white females 50–60 years of age	
Free white females 60–70 years of age	
Free white females 70–80 years of age	
Free white females 80–90 years of age	
Free white females 90–100 years of age	
Slaves	
Free colored people	
Deaf and dumb	
Blind	
Foreigners, not naturalized	

1850 US CENSUS

Census question	Person 1	Person 2	Person 3
Township or community			
County			
State			
Name of institution			
Name of incorporated place			
Enumeration date			
Enumerator			
Ward of city			
Supervisor's district			
Enumerator's district			
Written page number			
Printed page number			
Dwelling number			
Family number			
Name of every person whose usual place of abode 1 June 1850 was with this family			
Age			
Sex			
Color			
Profession, occupation, or trade of each male over 15			
Value of real estate owned			
Place of birth, naming state, territory, or county			
Married within the year			
In school within the year			
Persons over 20 unable to read and write			
Deaf and dumb, blind, insane, idiot, pauper, or convict			

1860 US CENSUS

Census question	Person 1	Person 2	Person 3
Township or community			
County			
State			
Name of institution			
Name of incorporated place			
Enumeration date			
Enumerator			
Ward of city			
Supervisor's district			
Enumerator's district			
Written page number			
Printed page number			
Dwelling number			
Family number			
Name of every person whose usual place of abode 1 June 1860 was with this family			
Age			
Sex			
Color			
Profession, occupation, or trade of each male over 15			
Value of real estate owned			
Place of birth, naming state, territory, or county			
Married within the year			
In school within the year			
Persons over 20 unable to read and write			
Deaf and dumb, blind, insane, idiot, pauper, or convict			

1870 US CENSUS

Census question	Person 1	Person 2	Person 3
Township or community			
County			
State			
Name of institution			
Name of incorporated place			
Enumeration date			
Enumerator			
Ward of city			
Supervisor's district			
Enumerator's district			
Written page number			
Printed page number			
Dwelling number			
Family number			
Name of every person whose usual place of abode 1 June 1870 was with this family			
Age			
Sex			
Color			
Profession, occupation, or trade of each male over 15			
Value of real estate owned			
Value of personal estate owned			
Place of birth			
Father foreign born			
Mother foreign born			
Month born in year			
Month married in year			

Census question	Person 1	Person 2	Person 3
In school within year			
Cannot read			
Cannot write			
Deaf, blind, insane			
Males able to vote			

1880 US CENSUS

Census question	Person 1	Person 2	Person 3
Township or community			
County			
State			
Name of institution			
Name of incorporated place			
Enumeration date			
Enumerator			
Ward of city			
Supervisor's district			
Enumerator's district			
Written page number			
Printed page number			
Dwelling number			
Family number			
Name of every person whose usual place of abode 1 June 1880 was with this family			
Color			
Sex			
Age			
Month born if during the census year			

Census question	Person 1	Person 2	Person 3
Relationship to head of household			
Single			
Married			
Widowed/divorced			
Married during year			
Profession, trade, or occupation			
Number of months unemployed			
Currently sick or disabled			
Blind, deaf and dumb, idiotic, insane, or disabled			
Attended school this year			
Cannot read			
Cannot write			
Birthplace			
Birthplace of father			
Birthplace of mother			

1900 US CENSUS

Census question	Person 1	Person 2	Person 3
Township or community			
County			
State			
Name of institution			
Name of incorporated place			
Enumeration date			
Enumerator			
Ward of city			
Supervisor's district			
Enumerator's district			

Census question	Person 1	Person 2	Person 3
Written page number			
Printed page number			
Dwelling number			
Family number			
Name of every person whose usual place of abode 1 June 1900 was with this family			
Relationship to head of family			
Color			
Sex			
Month of birth			
Year of birth			
Age			
Marital status			
Number of years married			
Mother of how many children?			
Number of children living			
Place of birth			
Father's place of birth			
Mother's place of birth			
Year of immigration			
Number of years in the United States			
Naturalized citizen			
Occupation of every person 10 and older			
Number of months unemployed			
Number of months in school			
Can read			
Can write			
Can speak English			

Census question	Person 1	Person 2	Person 3
Owned or rented			
Own free and clear or mortgaged			
Farm or house			

1910 US CENSUS

Census question	Person 1	Person 2	Person 3
Township or community			
County			
State			
Name of institution			
Name of incorporated place			
Enumeration date			
Enumerator			
Ward of city			
Supervisor's district			
Enumerator's district			
Sheet number			
Line number			
House number			
Dwelling number			
Number of family			
Name of every person living in this family on 15 April 1910			
Relationship to head of household			
Sex			
Color or race			
Age at last birthday			
Single, married, widowed, or divorced			

Census question	Person 1	Person 2	Person 3
Years of present marriage			
Number of children born to this mother			
Number of children still living			
Place of birth			
Father's place of birth			
Mother's place of birth			
Year immigrated to the United States			
Naturalized or alien			
Able to speak English or language spoken			
Trade or profession			
General nature of industry, business, or establishment			
Employer, employee, or self			
Out of work on 15 April 1910			
Weeks out of work in 1909			
Can speak English			
Able to read			
Able to write			
Attended school since 1 September			
Owned or rented			
Owned free, or mortgaged			
Farm or house			
Number of farm schedule			
Survivor Union or Confederate Army/Navy			
Blind in both eyes			
Deaf and dumb			

1920 US CENSUS

Census question	Person 1	Person 2	Person 3
Township or community			
County			
State			
Name of institution			
Name of incorporated place			
Enumeration date			
Enumerator			
Ward of city			
Supervisor's district			
Enumerator's district			
Sheet number			
Line number			
Street address			
House number or farm number			
Number of dwelling house			
Number of family			
Name of every person living in this family as of 1 January 1920			
Relationship to head of household			
Home owned or rented			
If owned, free or mortgaged			
Sex			
Color or race			
Age at last birthday			
Single, married, widowed, or divorced			
Year of immigration to the United States			
Naturalized or alien			

Unofficial Ancestry.com Workbook

Census question	Person 1	Person 2	Person 3
If naturalized, which year			
Attended school since 1 September			
Able to read			
Able to write			
Place of birth			
Mother tongue			
Place of birth of father			
Mother tongue of father			
Place of birth of mother			
Mother tongue of mother			
Able to speak English			
Trade or profession			
Type of business			
Employer, employee, or works for self			
Number of farm schedule			

1930 US CENSUS

Census question	Person 1	Person 2	Person 3
Township or community			
County			
State			
Name of institution			
Name of incorporated place			
Enumeration date			
Enumerator			
Ward of city			
Supervisor's district			
Enumerator's district			

Census question	Person 1	Person 2	Person 3
Sheet number			
Line number			
Street, avenue, road, etc.			
House number			
Dwelling number			
Number of family			
Name of every person living in this family as of 1 April 1930			
Relationship to head of household			
Home owned or rented			
Value of home, or monthly rent			
Radio set (leave blank if no radio)			
Does this family live on a farm?			
Sex			
Color or race			
Age at last birthday			
Marital condition			
Age at first marriage			
Attended school since 1 September			
Whether able to read and write			
Place of birth			
Place of birth of father			
Place of birth of mother			
Language spoken before arrival in the United States			
Year of immigration to United States			
Naturalization status			
Whether able to speak English			
Occupation, trade, or profession			
Industry or business			

Census question	Person 1	Person 2	Person 3
Class of worker			
Whether worked last working day			
Unemployment schedule line number			
Veteran of military or navy			
Served in what war/expedition			
Number of farm schedule			

1940 US CENSUS

Census question	Person 1	Person 2	Person 3
Township or community			
County			
State			
Name of institution			
Name of incorporated place			
Enumeration date			
Enumerator			
Ward of city			
Supervisor's district			
Enumerator's district			
Sheet number			
Line number			
Street, avenue, road, etc.			
House number			
Number of household			
Home owned or rented			
Value of home or monthly rent			
Farm (yes or no)			
Name of each person living in this family as of 1 April 1940			

Census question	Person 1	Person 2	Person 3
Relationship to head of household			
Sex			
Color or race			
Age at last birthday			
Marital status			
Attended school since 1 March 1940			
Highest grade of school completed			
Place of birth			
Citizenship, if foreign-born			
City or town of residence on 1 April 1935			
Country of residence on 1 April 1935			
State or country of residence on 1 April 1935			
Farm (yes or no)			
Working in non-government job the week of 24 March 1940			
If not, working in government job the week of 24 March 1940?			
If unemployed, seeking work?			
If unemployed and not seeking work, did he have a job/business?			
Engaged in housework, schoolwork, unable to work, or other?			
Number of hours worked during week of 24 March 1940?			
Duration of unemployment of 30 March 1940, in weeks			
Occupation, trade, or particular			
Kind of work			
Industry or business			
Class of worker			
Number of weeks worked in 1939			
Wages or salary received			

Census question	Person 1	Person 2	Person 3
Earned non-wage or salary income over $50			
Number of farm schedule			
Supplementary questions (asked only of people on lines 14 and 29)			
Place of birth of father			
Place of birth of mother			
Language spoken in home in earliest childhood			
Veteran?			
If child, is veteran-father dead?			
War or military service			
Social Security number issued			
Deductions for Federal Old Age Insurance or Railroad Retirement made?			
Deductions made from less than half, half, or more than half of wages?			
Usual occupation			
Usual industry			
Usual class of worker			
For women—married more than once?			
Age at first marriage			
Number of children ever born (excluding stillbirths)			

INDEX

ACKNOWLEDGMENTS

My thanks to the many genealogy enthusiasts who've written me over the years, sharing both their challenges and their successes. As a writer who loves delving into deep research problems, I have to admit that I can become a bit of a hermit. That's what makes hearing from readers or visitors to my website so special as it reminds me that there's life outside a computer screen. Keep writing—I love hearing from you!

Thanks, too, to Phyllis Quarg, Past-President of the San Diego Genealogical Society. Phyllis is my go-to person when I hit a brick wall as she always has a new perspective that helps me rethink genealogy problems. Years ago, she instilled in me a love of land records that I have to this day.

And of course a hat tip to publisher Allison Dolan and editor Andrew Koch. It was Allison who first had the idea for this book and Andrew who tidied up my penchant for writing never-ending sentences.

Finally, my deepest thanks to family, both past and present. Their stories inspire, their sense of adventure spurs me on, and their grittiness in the face of life's tragedies gives me courage. For me, genealogy research—in the end—is simply my attempt to know who I am.

DEDICATION

To the memory of my aunt, Helen Hendrickson Hjetland. She knew all the good stories.

ABOUT THE AUTHOR

Nancy Hendrickson is a genealogy author, blogger, and instructor at Ancestor News **<www.ancestornews. com>**, a site dedicated to finding and preserving family stories. A contributing editor at *Family Tree Magazine*, Nancy writes almost exclusively about Internet genealogy, research and American history. She's a member of Western Writers of America and a long-time photography buff. Nancy is active on Facebook **<www.facebook.com/genealogyteach>**, Twitter (*@genealogyteach*) and Pinterest **<www.pinterest.com/ genealogyteach>**. Her e-mail is *genealogyteach@gmail.com*.

UNOFFICIAL ANCESTRY.COM WORKBOOK: A HOW-TO MANUAL FOR TRACING YOUR FAMILY TREE ON THE NUMBER-ONE GENEALOGY WEBSITE.

Copyright © 2017 by Nancy Hendrickson. Manufactured in the United States of America. All rights reserved. No part of this book may be reproduced in any form or by any electronic or mechanical means including information storage and retrieval systems without permission in writing from the publisher, except by a reviewer, who may quote brief passages in a review. Published by Family Tree Books, an imprint of F+W Media, Inc., 10151 Carver Road, Suite 200, Blue Ash, Ohio 45242. (800) 289-0963. First edition. All other trademarks are property of their respective owners. This book is not authorized or sponsored by Ancestry.com or any other person or entity owning or controlling rights to Ancestry.com, its name, trademark, or copyrights. This guide has not been reviewed, edited, or approved by Ancestry.com or any of its employees or affiliates. The content of this book has been thoroughly reviewed for accuracy; however, the author and the publisher disclaim any liability for any damages or losses that may result from the misuse of any product or information presented herein. Readers should note that websites featured in this work may have changed between when the book was written and when it was read; always verify with the most recent information.

ISBN: 978-1-4403-4906-5

Other Family Tree Books are available from your local bookstore and online suppliers. For more genealogy resources, visit **<shopfamilytree.com>**.

21 20 19 18 17   5 4 3 2 1

DISTRIBUTED IN CANADA BY FRASER DIRECT

100 Armstrong Avenue

Georgetown, Ontario, Canada L7G 5S4

Tel: (905) 877-4411

DISTRIBUTED IN THE U.K. AND EUROPE BY

F&W Media International, LTD

Brunel House, Forde Close,

Newton Abbot, TQ12 4PU, UK

Tel: (+44) 1626 323200,

Fax (+44) 1626 323319

E-mail: enquiries@fwmedia.com

fw
a content + ecommerce company

PUBLISHER AND COMMUNITY LEADER: Allison Dolan

EDITOR: Andrew Koch

DESIGNER: Julie Barnett

PRODUCTION COORDINATOR: Debbie Thomas

4 FREE
FAMILY TREE templates

- decorative family tree posters
- five-generation ancestor chart
- family group sheet
- bonus relationship chart
- type and save, or print and fill out

Download at <ftu.familytreemagazine.com/free-family-tree-templates>

MORE GREAT GENEALOGY RESOURCES

FAMILY TREE MEMORY KEEPER

By the Editors of Family Tree Magazine

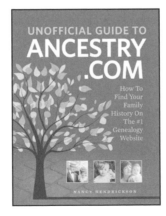

UNOFFICIAL GUIDE TO ANCESTRY.COM

By Nancy Hendrickson

ORGANIZE YOUR GENEALOGY

By Drew Smith

Available from your favorite bookstore, online booksellers and <shopfamilytree.com>, or by calling (855) 278-0408.

 Join our community! <facebook.com/familytreemagazine>